SHAKE FREE

SHAKE FREE

How to Deal with the Storms, Shipwrecks, and Snakes in Your Life

SAMUEL RODRIGUEZ

WATERBROOK

UNCORRECTED PROOF

Hardcover ISBN 978-1-60142-819-6
eBook ISBN 978-1-60142-820-2

Published in the United States by WaterBrook, an imprint of the Crown Publishing Group, a division of Penguin Random House LLC, New York.

WATERBROOK® and its deer colophon are registered trademarks of Penguin Random House LLC.

The Cataloging-in-Publication Data is on file with the Library of Congress.

Printed in the United States of America
2018—First Edition

10 9 8 7 6 5 4 3 2 1

SPECIAL SALES
Most WaterBrook books are available at special quantity discounts when purchased in bulk by corporations, organizations, and special-interest groups. Custom imprinting or excerpting can also be done to fit special needs. For information, please e-mail specialmarketscms@penguinrandomhouse.com or call 1-800-603-7051.

I dedicate this book to my entire New Season Church family. Pastoring and leading this Christ-centered, Bible-based, Spirit-empowered, multiethnic, multigenerational community of Christ followers is one of the great honors of my life. You continue to make me a better man, husband, father, and pastor, and your passionate faith is, I pray, reflected on every page of this book.

Contents

Foreword

Text to come.

1

On Your Way

In the middle of the journey of our life
I came to myself within a dark wood
where the straight way was lost.

—**Dante Alighieri**, *The Inferno*

couldn't believe where I was and what I was doing.

Although I had stood at many different podiums around the world and of-fered many prayers, both silently in the pew as well as publicly from the pulpit, this time was different. This time the eyes of the world were upon me as I took center stage on the platform only a few feet away from the president-elect just moments before he would become our nation's leader. A vast sea of faces from the hundreds of thousands in attendance at the inauguration looked up at me beneath luminous pewter-colored clouds. As I made my way to the po dium on this mild, damp January morning, I shivered despite my gray over-coat, more from being nervous than from the weather.

Taking a deep breath, I paused to celebrate all that God had done in my life to bring me to that moment. There I was—a Puerto Rican computer geek from Bethlehem, Pennsylvania—standing before millions of viewers in the very spot where Chief Justice John Roberts would soon swear in the president of the United States. Back in high school I was more concerned with the next Star Trek movie than anything to do with ministry. Never in a million years would I ever have imagined myself a pastor, let alone one about to deliver a prayer for our nation's new president at his inauguration!

Although I had been involved in several nonpartisan meetings with previous presidents, I was about to make history as the first Hispanic evangelical pastor to pray at this historic and prestigious event. Humbled to be there, I delivered the prayer derived from Scripture that God had placed on my heart and knew this moment was as monumental for me as for our new leader. Months, if not years, had led to where we each stood. After a grueling campaign and divisive election, the president would now move forward to unite us as one nation under God.

My route had also been a long, arduous journey, filled with more ups and downs than any roller coaster ride. (I'll tell you more about some of those later.) But then, isn't that true for all of us on our journeys of faith? Some days it feels as if we take one step forward and two steps back before we experience God's guidance toward the destination where he wants to take us. Sometimes we may even wonder whether we're going the right direction or whether we'll ever get where we believe we're supposed to be. We feel overwhelmed by and underequipped for life's storms and struggle to push through one obstacle, only to discover another larger one looming before us.

In other words, we feel just like the apostle Paul boarding a ship.

GETTING THERE

"Are we there yet?"

Like most parents, if I had a dollar for every time one of my kids asked that inevitable question while traveling, I'd have a pile of money. But children aren't the only ones who get impatient. Every time I board a plane, I check my watch and wonder whether my flight will be on time—the first of many such calculations. When delays leave me sitting on the tarmac along with dozens of other frustrated, impatient passengers, I try to remember the journey Paul took in order to get to Rome.

As we will see, this trip was anything but simple. And even if Paul didn't expect smooth sailing, I doubt he imagined anything like what actually occurred on his epic journey. Filled with an arrest, a trial, a life-threatening storm, a shipwreck, and a snakebite, Paul's path to Rome featured more drama than a reality TV show. Surely there were times when he had to wonder whether he would ever reach the capital of the Roman Empire. Maybe he questioned whether he had misunderstood what God wanted him to do or how God wanted him to do it or whether he had lost his sense of direction somewhere along the way.

Perhaps Paul's commitment to walking by faith despite his circumstances resulted from the dramatic upheaval he experienced in his life after encountering Christ. You see, Paul had once been known as Saul before he ran into Jesus while traveling on the road to Damascus. Raised in a strict Jewish home, Saul believed a person's righteousness could be achieved only by strictly following God's law. Consequently, Saul thought he and other Jews like him were the only ones worthy of God's favor because of how hard they worked to follow every commandment and obey every rule.

But Jesus came to fulfill the law and deliver all people—including you and me—from their sins once and for all. His gospel message of grace ran counter to virtually everything Saul, a strict Jew, had been taught and practiced his entire life. This explains why Saul persecuted the early followers of Jesus; he considered them heretics because they were going around telling everyone about grace and forgiveness in the name of Jesus Christ.

After his personal encounter with Jesus, however, Saul began doing the very thing he had once so violently opposed: spreading the good news beyond Israel by traveling and preaching to Gentiles in foreign lands. Along the way, he also began going by the Roman version of his name, Paul, both to show the change in his identity and to escape his reputation as a persecutor of Christians. Throughout his travels, Paul often wrote letters to the communities of believers in these distant locations, and many of these divinely inspired messages became part of what we call the New Testament.

We also know a lot about Paul's life from the narrative we find in the book of Acts, which most scholars believe was written by the same author as the gospel of Luke. Consequently, Paul emerges as a superhero of the Christian faith who continues to instruct us, inspire us, and ignite our hearts toward God today. As we will discover throughout these pages, Paul faced more pulse-pounding, life-or-death, cliff-hanger situations than Indiana Jones and Jason Bourne combined! From angry mobs eager to kill him to shipwrecks and jail cells, Paul faced each new trial with patience and faith.

WHEN IN ROME

Throughout all these twists and turns, however, Paul knew he would eventually get to Rome because that's where God wanted him to be. Far from being a vacation destination, the center of the Roman Empire was probably one of the most dangerous places in the world for Paul. Now known as the Eternal City because of its ties to ancient history and its timeless works of art and architecture, in Paul's day Rome was not only the capital but also the center of the most powerful military empire on the planet.

Consequently, Rome served as the United Nations of the early first century because of its diverse population, a result of the expansive conquests of so many tribes and nations. England, Spain, Syria, Israel, and much of what we now know as Western Europe and North Africa all belonged within Rome's grasp. At the time, all roads literally led to Rome.

Paul was on his way to Rome for a much more unusual reason than most of the international travelers of his day. He was en route to Rome because God wanted him to have a larger platform to amplify the narrative of this new faith known as "The Way," the early name for the beliefs of those following Jesus. But Paul was not going under the best of circumstances. In fact, on the surface they look like the *worst* of circumstances.

He wasn't going on vacation aboard a Royal Caribbean cruise ship or enjoying sunset views of the Mediterranean from the deck of a yacht or even a fishing boat. No, Paul sailed for Rome as an inmate on a prison ship! Arrested for creating a disturbance in Jerusalem, Paul went before a council of leaders only to be found not guilty (see Acts 25–26). Because so many of his fellow Jews continued to harass him, he nonetheless asked to go before the Roman courts to put the matter to rest once and for all.

We don't know for sure, but I suspect Paul also wanted the opportunity to share the gospel with such an influential political audience. Regardless of his motives, Paul continues to serve as an incredible example to us today of someone willing to go the extra mile—or in this case all 1,433 of them, the distance from Jerusalem to Rome as the crow flies—to advance God's kingdom. No matter how rough the sailing or how impossible the situation, Paul refused to give up his firm belief that God was still in charge. Paul knew he would eventually get to Rome one way or another.

YOU'RE GOING TO MAKE IT

Paul's journey to Rome inspires us to persevere no matter what life throws at us or how big the obstacles appear that block our paths. You may never have been to Rome, but I'm guessing you've encountered enough storms in life to know that the sailing is seldom smooth for long. Maybe it's because we're all plugged in and connected by social media, but it feels as though our world is a scarier, more dangerous place than ever. Hurricanes and wildfires. Horrific mass shootings and terrorist attacks. Economic downturns and corporate layoffs.

And beneath all the headlines and sound bites are the lives of families, men and women, children and teens, trying to keep going in the midst of each crisis or disaster. Trying to get through another day while grappling with the pain of a lost loved one, a home destroyed, or a job terminated. Working to keep food on the table, catch up on overdue bills, and support ailing parents. Fighting to not give in to discouragement and despair, to the unfairness and injustice all around them.

If I've learned anything during the past two decades of being a pastor, it's that you never know what another person is going through. Most days this awareness motivates me to be kinder to my waitress or more patient with the driver in front of me (quite a feat in California!). But then sometimes my own struggles and weariness consume my attention and I lose sight of the pain of others. I begin to long for heaven with renewed vigor, eager to escape the latest crisis or the daily struggle.

Those are the moments when, just like my kids on a long trip, I ask, "How much longer? Are we there yet?" And then God reminds me, often in some surprising way, of his love, his concern, and his presence. My hope is that this book will be one of those uplifting and unexpectedly refreshing encounters, a way for God to speak in your life and whisper, *Keep going! You're on your way and I'm still with you. You're going to make it to Rome, no matter how impossible it looks right now.*

YOU ARE HERE

Sometimes we look at individuals in the Bible as far removed from our present, everyday struggles to work hard, push through, and keep our families together. But I doubt any of them felt any differently than you and I feel when trouble came knocking on their doors. Maybe that's one of the reasons Paul compiled a list of great men and women of faith to encourage other believers.

While some scholars question the authorship of the New Testament book we call Hebrews, I believe Paul wrote it. He knew that all the saints listed in the great Faith Hall of Fame, found in Hebrews 11, probably faced the same feelings, thoughts, doubts, and worries that you and I have faced or may be facing right now. He knew that they were just as human as anyone else yet were willing to trust God in their painful, crazy, uncertain struggles. They were willing to keep getting up every time they got knocked down.

In this passage Paul was not simply defining faith but was showing us examples of faith in action. He understood the big difference between knowing something in theory and experiencing it personally, between hearing it taught once or twice and living it out every day. In writing to other early followers of Jesus, Paul wanted them to persevere in their faith no matter what their circumstances might be. He knew all too well how hard trials can seem and how challenging it becomes to trust God when life goes sideways and our expectations go unmet.

Paul reminds us that it was just as hard for all those great pioneers of our faith. It's easy for us to assume that Noah's bedrock faith empowered his confidence to build the ark without a cloud in the sky. But it must have been really tough listening to all his friends and neighbors mock him and laugh at what they considered crazy behavior.

I suspect it was the same with Ruth and Naomi. Why in the world should Ruth leave her home and everything familiar—especially after losing her husband unexpectedly—to follow her bitter mother-in-law, Naomi? It's easy to admire Ruth's faith after the fact because we know that Boaz was waiting to marry her in a happily-ever-after ending in Bethlehem. But during that long, dusty journey from Moab to Israel, Ruth probably had her doubts.

Or consider Job. If anyone deserved to give in to doubt and give up on God, surely he's at the top of the list. Job endured just about every loss imaginable: his children, his wealth, his wife, and his health. Still he refused to blame

God and instead clung stubbornly to the irrational belief that his Creator loved him and had not forsaken him, even when everyone around him thought otherwise. I certainly hope you haven't lost as much as Job did, but I'm guessing you've felt the same intensity of grief, anger, and fear that he may have felt.

You may not consider your faith to be as strong as that of these heroes of our faith, but it is. It simply takes a willingness to keep going during life's ups and downs, to trust God when you can't understand what he's up to. This is what "going to Rome" is all about—staying the course to follow God through the many trials, temptations, and tangents of your life. Trusting that he has your best interests at heart as he leads you forward. Glimpsing eternity and your home with him through the peace, joy, and satisfaction that comes from reaching your ultimate destination.

Maybe this sounds good but you're still struggling to imagine it applied to your own life. Whether you consider your life stalled by a dead end, derailed by a detour, or blocked by unexpected obstacles, I can promise you two things: you're not alone and your journey is far from over.

No matter where you are, God is there with you.

You might feel as though you've lost your way and are wandering alone in the wilderness. Years ago you walked with God and trusted him to guide your steps, but then something happened and you stumbled away from him. Now you wonder whether you're ever going to find your way back. Perhaps you experienced the ordeal of losing a loved one unexpectedly and your grief continues to burden your heart. Maybe you ache to have children but haven't been blessed yet to add little ones to your family. Or it could be the stress of raising kids as a single parent, trying to keep them safe and secure in a fast-moving, online world.

No matter where you are, though, God is there with you. In his Word, he promises us his presence throughout all that we experience: "The LORD himself goes before you and will be with you; he will never leave you nor forsake you. Do not be afraid; do not be discouraged" (Deuteronomy 31:8). The psalmist even reminds us that no matter where life's journey may take us, we will never be separated from God:

> Where can I go from your Spirit?
>> Where can I flee from your presence?
> If I go up to the heavens, you are there;
>> if I make my bed in the depths, you are there.
> If I rise on the wings of the dawn,
>> if I settle on the far side of the sea,
> even there your hand will guide me,
>> your right hand will hold me fast. (Psalm 139:7–10)

God knows where you are and has never left you, regardless of how you may feel or how uncertain you are of where you're going. It reminds me of when our kids were small and we visited Disneyland for the first time. The park was so big and probably seemed enormous to our three children. After wandering around for a few hours, we wanted to find our way back to Cinderella's castle near the entrance. In our pre-GPS world, I thought I knew the way but ended up taking us to Space Mountain instead. The kids began to worry that we'd never find our way back. Then my son grabbed my hand and pulled me over to a giant map of the park—you know, the kind with the big arrow pointing "You Are Here."

Suddenly it was easy to regain our perspective and see how we needed to proceed in order to get to our destination. We hadn't really been lost, of course; we just couldn't see where we were in relation to where we wanted to go.

The same is true for you. Whether you feel as if you're blazing a trail in the wilderness or maintaining a predictable plateau, God knows where you are and where you're going. He's right there with you and has big plans for where he wants to take you. If you feel lost, stuck, or caught in a rut, consider this: When was the last time you stopped to ask him for directions?

PACK YOUR BAGS

Paul knew firsthand what it meant to experience God's loving presence in all circumstances. No wonder he wrote to the early church in Rome with such confidence, "Can anything ever separate us from Christ's love? Does it mean he no longer loves us if we have trouble or calamity, or are persecuted, or hungry, or destitute, or in danger, or threatened with death? . . . No, despite all these things, overwhelming victory is ours through Christ, who loved us" (Romans 8:35, 37, NLT).

We often don't recognize the journey we're on or the route we've taken until we look back. And rarely do we take the most direct route. But regardless of our ability to see clearly how we'll get there, we can trust that God will make a way.

No matter how far away from God you may have wandered or how long you've been faithfully following him, you are on your way to something bigger, better, and more blessed than where you are right now. Your Rome may seem like a distant, impossible dream that has sputtered and turned to ash. But God knows that dream because he gave it to you and created you for the specific purpose of its fulfillment. He will make sure you reach Rome if you'll only follow him.

Everything you've experienced so far in your life has brought you to this moment. And God can use all of it to equip you for where you're going. Nothing is wasted in God's economy, and he can redeem even your greatest mistakes and most shameful secrets. But you have to let him! If you're not following him, you have to make a U-turn and go back to letting him lead the way. If you're already following him, you are about to grow closer to him and experience a more confident trust in his goodness, power, and sovereignty.

You may be in Des Moines, Dallas, Detroit, or Daytona.

You might be in the Australian Outback or the frozen tundra of Alaska.

You might be going through a divorce or looking for another job.

You could be recovering from an injury or battling an addiction.

You might feel lost or you might feel found.

No matter where you are or how you feel, it's time to pack your bags and get ready—because if you're willing to trust God and follow him, you're going to Rome!

Shake Free . . . from Settling for Less

At the end of each chapter, you will find several questions for you to think about and apply to your own life. You don't have to write your answers down, but you might be surprised how helpful it can be if you do. After you've spent a few moments sitting with these questions and considering your responses, talk to God about what's going on inside you. You'll find a short prayer after the questions to facilitate this conversation.

1. Where are you on your life's journey right now? How would you describe the route your life has taken? A routine ride on a city bus? Galloping horseback through the Wild West? Sailing through stormy seas? How does where you are compare with where you want to be?

2. How would you describe your relationship with God presently?
   Day in and day out, how willing are you to trust him to guide you?
   What past experiences are eroding your faith and impeding your
   willingness to trust him? What do you need to talk about with him?

_____

Dear God, I never really imagined myself where I am right now. While I know the events and choices that brought me here, I still wonder how I got here and, more importantly, if this is where I'm supposed to be. Somehow I know there's more. I believe you created me for more joy, peace, and purpose than I'm experiencing in my life right now. I want to trust you and believe that the best is yet to come, that I will get to Rome one day. Thank you for accepting me where I am, Lord, and for loving me enough to send your Son to die for me on the cross. I'm willing to follow you, beginning right now, today. Amen.

2

Perception Is Not Reality

There are things known and there are
things unknown, and in between are
the doors of perception.

—attributed to Aldous Huxley

Early in my ministry I faced a test of faith that cut straight to my heart—as a pastor, as a father, and, ultimately, as a believer. Perhaps more than any other event I can recall, it taught me that believing doesn't depend on seeing. As Dr. Martin Luther King Jr. has been famously quoted as saying, "Faith is taking the first step, even when you don't see the whole staircase."

As I discovered, it's one thing to walk down a staircase in the dark when you're familiar with it and know where it leads. It's another to keep taking step after step when you feel as if there's no staircase at all.

This event happened when my wife, Eva, and I had been married only a few years. We had recently started our family, grateful to be blessed with a beautiful baby girl, whom we named Yvonne, followed by our son, Nathan, and another beautiful daughter, Lauren. At the time, we were living near my parents in Pennsylvania, where I served as a youth pastor at a small church in the Allentown area. Though I remained surprised I was a pastor, I was experiencing the joy of the Lord as I learned to lead and pour myself into so many young lives. Despite my mechanically inclined mind and love of computers, I knew I was where God wanted me to be.

Then little Yvonne got sick. Her aunt, just home from a mission trip to the Dominican Republic, had come to visit us and apparently had a virus that she passed along to her niece. Because her auntie got over the bug in a few days, we weren't alarmed at first. Parents never like to see their child feeling poorly, so Eva and I did all we could and assumed Yvonne would bounce back just as quickly as her aunt had.

Instead of getting better in a few days, however, our daughter became much worse. Pale and lifeless, she ran a fever and continued to weaken. She had no appetite and fidgeted in her sleep. When we took her to the doctor, he couldn't identify the exact cause of her illness and insisted she be admitted immediately to the hospital. Needless to say, our concern jumped to the critical level.

As preliminary tests failed to deliver a diagnosis and treatment, Eva and I tried not to panic. We prayed together and took comfort from family and friends who came to support us. But when Yvonne's condition continued to deteriorate instead of improve, I silently began to question God. Why in the world would he allow this precious, innocent child to suffer like this? And why couldn't the doctors figure out what was wrong so they could treat her and heal her? It simply didn't make sense.

I'll never forget seeing all the tubes in my little girl and hearing the monitors buzzing and beeping around her. She looked so tiny and vulnerable in that big hospital bed. I wanted to do something—*anything*—to see her smile again, to hear her laugh when I tickled her, to feel her little hand in mine. I prayed and prayed, pouring my heart out to God to restore my daughter. In return, I heard . . . nothing. While I knew God was with me, I felt terribly alone.

After several more days with no improvement in Yvonne and no diagnosis of her mystery illness, her doctors called the Centers for Disease Control and

Prevention in Atlanta, the national hub for monitoring and preventing infectious diseases. By this time, the nurses and doctors were taking extra precautions and wearing hazmat-type suits when they entered Yvonne's room. We had to do the same thing, which made the experience more surreal.

After talking to her doctors late one afternoon, I no longer could keep the terrible thought rolling around in my head at bay: *What if we lose her? What if our daughter dies?*

Exhausted from lack of sleep and raw with emotion, I seriously began to doubt God for the first time in my life. Growing up in a healthy, happy Christian home, I had not struggled to believe in God or welcome Jesus into my life. My parents and others in our church had modeled what it meant to love God and serve others. Faith made sense to me. And as my faith grew, I trusted God with more and more of my life—to the point where I had answered his call to enter full-time ministry.

Yvonne's illness threatened all that, and within a week's time, I was questioning whether God was really there. Whether or not he cared—about me, about our suffering little girl, about any of us. Even from my limited time as a pastor, I knew it wasn't just our family who dealt with suffering, but now the experience was real and personal.

Where was God? And why wasn't he doing something for my daughter?

I WANT TO BELIEVE

Days dragged on like weeks as we rode the roller coaster of possible diagnoses and tentative treatments. I went through the motions of praying and hoping, uncertain and at times afraid. I wanted to trust God with my baby girl's life, but it required so much and left me feeling so vulnerable. Finally, by the second week of her hospitalization, my prayers began to be answered. Doctors concluded that our daughter's six-year-old immune system couldn't handle the bug that her aunt had unknowingly passed on to her. But with a combination of high-powered antibiotics and other treatments, Yvonne's body won the fight and overcame her mystery disease.

I'm delighted to tell you that Yvonne eventually made a full recovery. I've never been more grateful to God for anything in my life.

The memory of this ordeal still causes my soul to wince in pain. I don't know how I would have kept going if God had allowed Yvonne to leave this earth at such a young age. Honestly, I don't know how parents endure such pain while coping with a child's permanent injuries, lifelong disabilities, or even death.

I didn't lose my faith during Yvonne's illness, but I've never had it stretched so thin. And while I don't know why my little girl had to go through this painful battle, I trust that God knows. As shattered as I was, I clung to the only shred of truth that made sense at the time: *there's more going on here than I can comprehend.* Somehow I had to trust that God was still in control—even if the very worst happened—and not try to make sense of it from my limited human point of view. I assure you, this is easier said than done.

Have you endured your own trials that shook your faith? Whether it's a sick child, an aging parent's dementia, a lost job, or a secret addiction, sooner or later we all encounter the crossroads of calamity. At those junctures we have to make a choice about what we believe, who we trust, and which direction we're going to go. To put it simply, we have to decide whether our faith is real.

Through these various battles of faith, however, we can be sure there's more going on than meets the eye. In the moment we can see only the enormous debt, the unexpected diagnosis, the heartbreaking betrayal, or the crippling loss. But as followers of Jesus, we must never forget there's an invisible reality beyond what we can see. God is at work even when it doesn't look like it. And that's when we have an opportunity to grow in our faith and discover whether we're really serious about what we say we believe.

Our struggle to believe is nothing new. After his resurrection Jesus visited his disciples and offered Thomas, the skeptic, an opportunity to place his fingers in the nail holes of Christ's hands—which is what Thomas had said it would take for him to believe that his Master had actually risen from the tomb (see John 20:25). Jesus wanted Thomas to "stop doubting and believe" (verse 27). Then Jesus went on to make a point about the essence of true faith, about the difference between seeing and believing: "Because you have seen me, you have believed; blessed are those who have not seen and yet have believed" (verse 29).

> ## We must never forget there's an invisible reality beyond what we can see.

I'm convinced that learning to walk by faith—and to keep going and persevering and following God even when circumstances close in around us—is essential to becoming who God wants us to be. My history-making visit to Washington, DC, on Inauguration Day wasn't where I expected to be, but it was the culmination of many little steps of faith over many years—including those days and nights on my knees pleading for God to heal Yvonne.

Even then God knew where he was taking me and how to get me there.

Even when I couldn't see it or even imagine it, God led me each step of the way.

Even when I wasn't sure I could keep going.

So no matter where you may find yourself right now—in a dead-end job or a struggling marriage, battling an addiction, or grieving a rebellious child—just remember you can't see all that God is doing in your life and where he wants to take you.

SEEING AND BELIEVING

From childhood on, we constantly wrestle with the tension between what we think we see and the truth concealed beneath the surface. It doesn't take too many years for us to grasp that Santa Claus and the Tooth Fairy aren't real as we might once have believed. Magicians performing at other kids' birthday parties turn out not to be related to Harry Potter but are only skilled illusionists with clever props. Even our adolescent infatuations drive this lesson home as we see our romantic fantasies shattered by the selfish realities of fickle peers.

And our education in appearances doesn't end at childhood. A house that looks HGTV perfect when we move in turns out to be *This Old House,* immediately transforming from our dream home into a money pit. Friendly co-workers we thought we could trust soon reveal themselves to be backstabbing rivals for the next promotion. Even beloved family members can betray us, leaving us to wonder whether we can ever know who they truly are.

Conversely, painful events, unpredictable people, and challenging circumstances sometimes ignite positive change beyond what we can see at the time. If you hadn't lost your job when you did, you wouldn't have found the great employer you have now. If your fiancé hadn't broken up with you, you would not have met and married the man who became your husband. If you hadn't endured chemotherapy and beaten cancer, you wouldn't have committed to a healthier lifestyle.

Perhaps nowhere is this tension more apparent than in our spiritual lives. In fact, the very essence of faith is believing in that which cannot be seen and discerned by human eyes and mortal minds. The Bible explains, "Faith shows the reality of what we hope for; it is the evidence of things we cannot see" (Hebrews 11:1, NLT). Faith requires us to put our perceptions aside and rely instead on the truth of God's promises and our trust in his goodness, power, and sovereignty—which I admit is extremely difficult when we are going through excruciating circumstances.

Yet those very circumstances are often when our faith matters most, because that's when we can expect God to do the impossible. That's when we learn to shake free from false perceptions and cling to timeless truth. That's when we should get ready to meet our miracle!

FAITH IN 3-D

Like seeing a flat screen through 3-D glasses, we must learn to see beyond the momentary distractions and urgent dilemmas we face daily and focus on an eternal perspective. Understanding that our human perceptions are limited, we learn to see through the lens of faith, glimpsing God's reality as we trust him to guide us. Through this lens of faith, we learn to shake off the snares of the devil, the challenges of circumstances, the disappointment of unmet expectations, and the pain of loss. We shake free and break through to live with joy and purpose in the new life we have in Jesus Christ. That's what this book is all about.

When Scripture directly addresses this friction between what appears to be true and what is actually true, the apostle Paul is often the author. His entire life, in fact, provides us with a dramatic case study in surface perception versus depth of faith. Events and circumstances on the surface of his life often were chaotic, but underneath the surface, Paul's faithfulness in turmoil was being used by God to further his divine kingdom for eternity. Paul, like us, experienced his life from a limited, personal point of view. He knew his obedience to God didn't provide him with anything he didn't already have through Jesus Christ. But because of his trust in God and devotion to Christ, Paul knew there was much more going on beyond what he could see—something spiritual, invisible, and eternal.

REJOICE IN SUFFERING

I encounter so many Christians who erroneously assume that if they're obeying God and answering his call on their lives, everything will be easy and go smoothly. After all, Jesus told us he came so that we might have an abundant, contented, full life, right? But we mustn't overlook what Christ said just before that statement: "The thief comes only to steal and kill and destroy" (John 10:10). Jesus made a striking contrast, one that speaks directly to this tension between what we perceive and what is actually true.

Nowhere are we told that we can avoid and eliminate all trials, pain, persecution, and suffering if we obey God. On the contrary, we see so many examples in Scripture of just the opposite. We're told Job, for instance, "was blameless and upright; he feared God and shunned evil" (Job 1:1). Then why did Job suffer loss after loss? Because he caught the attention of both God, who held him up as an example of loving obedience, and Satan, the Enemy of our souls, who will do anything to drive a wedge between us and God.

After hearing the Lord comment on Job's faithfulness, Satan insinuated that the only reason Job remained obedient was because God rewarded him: "Have you not put a hedge around him and his household and everything he has? You have blessed the work of his hands, so that his flocks and herds are spread throughout the land. But now stretch out your hand and strike everything he has, and he will surely curse you to your face" (verses 10–11).

Satan implied that Job didn't really love God, that he was just doing what was necessary to get what he wanted. It's similar to the lie the Enemy continually tries to plant inside us today: "God doesn't really love you and want what's best for you. If he did, why would he allow you to suffer through all that you're facing right now?"

This evil logic appeals to our rational human minds because it plays to our experiences on earth, but our eternal lives are bigger than what we experience for a short time in mortal bodies. With our limited view and shortsightedness, we usually miss the big picture of what God is up to. We may view disappointments, crises, and trials as attacks by the devil, but I suspect usually they're merely the consequences of selfish choices in a sinful world.

Now, the Enemy will try to exploit our weaknesses and tempt us when we're struggling and more vulnerable. From Adam and Eve in the Garden of Eden to Jesus coming out of his forty-day fast in the desert, we see Satan repeatedly employing this strategy. God has a better plan: he not only gives us strength to resist but also redeems our trials by using them to make us stronger. They provide us with extraordinary opportunities to grow, learn, mature, and prepare ourselves for what lies ahead of us. And the more we're willing to seek God in the midst of our struggles, the better equipped we become to serve him moving forward.

> **With our limited view and shortsightedness, we usually miss the big picture of what God is up to.**

Paul experienced this reality firsthand. He said, "I only know that in every city the Holy Spirit warns me that prison and hardships are facing me" (Acts 20:23). Even though Paul knew his life was going to get harder, not easier, he learned to welcome these obstacles and hardships because he knew the fruit they could produce in his life: "But we also glory in our sufferings, because we know that suffering produces perseverance; perseverance, character; and character, hope" (Romans 5:3–4). As hard as it may be to accept when we're going through hard times, Paul encouraged us to "be joyful in hope, patient in affliction, faithful in prayer" (12:12).

And Paul wasn't the only one encouraging us to welcome trials as doorways for spiritual growth. James explained, "Consider it pure joy, my brothers and sisters, whenever you face trials of many kinds, because you know that the testing of your faith produces perseverance. Let perseverance finish its work so that you may be mature and complete, not lacking anything" (James 1:2–4).

It may not be easy to hear, but it's part of the reality we can't always see in the middle of our struggles. Just as muscles in our bodies must be used in order to stay healthy and strong, we can grow spiritually only when our faith is tested, stretched, and refined.

THORNY PROBLEMS

Instead of trying to look elsewhere for help or relief, or praying for an immediate escape hatch, we must learn to trust God no matter what we're experiencing. Even during our weakest moments—*especially* during our weakest moments—we can rely on our Father's strength to see us through.

Our inability to handle all that life throws at us is actually a gift because we're forced to depend on God. Our dependence isn't needed simply in moments of crisis; it's also needed when we're facing painful struggles and emotional battles that never seem to end. Paul struggled with a "thorn in [his] flesh" (2 Corinthians 12:7) that he asked God to remove, but it did not go away. Instead, Paul learned to see the value in his pain:

> [The Lord] said to me, "My grace is sufficient for you, for my power is
> made perfect in weakness." Therefore I will boast all the more gladly
> about my weaknesses, so that Christ's power may rest on me. That is
> why, for Christ's sake, I delight in weaknesses, in insults, in hardships,
> in persecutions, in difficulties. For when I am weak, then I am strong.
> (verses 9–10)

While you or I might have been disappointed and even angry that God didn't take away the thorn, Paul actually *rejoiced* in God's reply because he knew it meant he would be forced to continue relying on God. Sounds loco, right? But it's true. Paul couldn't remove this struggle or escape its pain, and God wouldn't remove it for him—which meant Paul had to live with this thorn and face it daily, persevering through all the other circumstances of his life. What Paul discovered remains an essential paradox of our Christian faith: *"When I am weak, then I am strong"* (verse 10).

What are you going through right now that's blurring your vision of reality?

What's weighing on you and distracting you from trusting God and walking by faith?

What thorn or weakness keeps cutting away at your soul?

Maybe you're worried about money and how you're going to pay your bills this month. Perhaps your marriage feels disappointing and unfulfilling as you and your spouse continue to grow apart. You might be suffering from a physical injury or disease that leaves you in constant pain and distress. Maybe you're battling an addiction that makes every day an excruciating ordeal as you try to resist using. It could be you're anxious about your kids and what they're facing at school.

Most of us have no shortage of worries weighing us down. But here's the deal, my friend: God uses circumstances that seem superficially egregious to show off his glory. He loves to come into situations that we view as hopeless and suddenly make the impossible possible. Whether it's parting the Red Sea to provide the ultimate escape route for his people out of Egypt or blessing a few loaves and fish to feed more than five thousand people, God loves to dazzle us with his power, provision, and peace.

REALITY CHECK

As our faith matures and we go through a few things with God, we learn to trust him more and more. In other words, when the going gets tough, the tough know that God is going to get a ton of glory! But based on surface appearances, we often make assumptions that fit with the physical, circumstantial evidence. Obstacles in our paths loom large and we can't imagine how we'll ever get around them. Hope is scarce and fear is abundant. The realm of the spirit is not visible to our eyes.

Even though we're made in God's image with eternal souls, we're limited in our mortal bodies. We get stuck on seeing only what is before our earthly eyes. But when we remember the truth, then we remember we can't see all that's going on in our lives. Let me say it again: *God uses circumstances that seem superficially egregious to show off his glory.*

From the perspective of the Romans, Paul was going to Rome to stand trial before the emperor. It was possible he would face execution if he wasn't murdered first by angry Jewish zealots. And of course, as we will see, traveling from Jerusalem to Rome wasn't a quick, one-day trip. From a human perspective, things looked really bad.

God's perspective was totally different, for he knew Paul was about to preach the gospel message on the most important stage of that time. The Lord appeared to him and said, "Be encouraged, Paul. Just as you have been a witness to me here in Jerusalem, you must preach the Good News in Rome as well" (Acts 23:11, NLT). Basically, God said, "I'm sending you to Rome to take my gospel global!" While most people perceived Paul's journey to be a life-threatening ordeal, in reality God had predestined Paul to go on a journey that would launch him into his anointed destiny, which would have eternal consequences.

The same is true for us today. Others around us think they know what will happen to us, and we often believe them. We allow our doctors, bosses, families, and friends to help us define what we're going through. Yet there's another reality below the surface: God's reality. This is the one that's ultimately true.

BUILT ON PROMISES

Just as Paul's journey to Rome revealed the vast difference between the seen and unseen, your human perception is not God's reality.

It may look as if it's too late for you to beat the cancer ravaging your body.

It may look as if it's beyond hope that you'll ever find another job.

It may look as if your marriage could never be restored.

It may look as if the devil is winning.

It may look as if hell is about to celebrate.

It may look as if you will never come out of what you are going through.

But perception is not reality!

No matter what it looks like, you're not seeing the complete picture. Even as you're reading these words, God is transforming your hardest, most painful circumstances into catalysts for growth and blessing.

God is for you, and when it's all said and done, what looked like your worst defeat will actually emerge as your greatest victory. What looked like your end will actually be your beginning. What you're going through right now is about to catapult you to where God wants to take you next.

Why am I so sure? It's not just because I've experienced it in my own life. It's not just because I've observed God do the impossible time and time again. It's because of the promises God gives us in his Word. Just consider a few of them that remind us to look beyond our perceptions in order to glimpse God's reality:

"For I know the plans I have for you," declares the LORD, "plans to prosper you and not to harm you, plans to give you hope and a future." (Jeremiah 29:11)

As it is written:

"What no eye has seen,
  what no ear has heard,
and what no human mind has conceived"—
    the things God has prepared for those who love him.
    (1 Corinthians 2:9, referencing Isaiah 64:4)

For the Lord Almighty has purposed, and who can thwart him?

His hand is stretched out, and who can turn it back?

(Isaiah 14:27)

You must understand that the Enemy attacks you not because of the foolish things you have done but *because of the glorious things you are about to do.* God has called each of us on a journey to Rome to live out his passionate purposes for which he created and equipped us.

> ## The Enemy attacks you not because of the foolish things you have done but *because of the glorious things you are about to do.*

No matter where you are right now, my friend, your story isn't over and your journey hasn't ended. God has a destination for you and has been preparing you your entire life for what's next. Shake free of mistakes and misperceptions about what you think is true in your life and replace them with God's truth. Your future is built on the promises of God and empowered by the Holy Spirit.

Don't live by what you perceive and what is going on around you. Simply trust God and know there's so much more happening that you can't see. Put perception in its place and live by faith, not by sight!

SHAKE FREE . . . FROM PERCEPTIONS

Use the following questions to help you consider ways you can live by faith and not by sight.

1. Can you think of past events that were painful at the time that you've now seen God transform or redeem in some way? How do you feel as you think about the difference between your perception then and the reality you can see now?

2. What's the greatest struggle you're experiencing right now? What is your perception of this "thorn in your flesh" and how it affects your life? What would you like to tell God about this struggle and your perception of it?

———————————————

*Dear God, there's so much on my mind right now. I'm tired of worrying and feeling so anxious all the time. Even though I want to believe there's another reality—**your** reality—taking place beyond what I can see, it's so hard to keep trusting and hoping. I need your help because I can't do this on my own. Please remind me of your presence and speak to my heart through your Holy Spirit. Give me strength, Lord, and help me see beyond my surface perception and trust you to guide me toward the reality of your power, love, and grace. Amen.*

3

Storm Driven or Destiny Driven?

Destiny is not a matter of chance; it is a
matter of choice; it is not a thing to be
waited for, it is a thing to be achieved.

—William Jennings Bryan, "America's
Mission" speech delivered February 22, 1899

G rowing up in Pennsylvania, I became a die-hard Pittsburgh Steelers fan—and I still am. As a little boy I watched the glory days of such Steelers legends as Terry Bradshaw, "Mean" Joe Greene (remember that Coke commercial? I wanted to be that kid!), Franco Harris, and Lynn Swann—all amazing athletes and now Hall of Famers.

Even though my blood runs black and gold, a few years ago I found myself doing the unthinkable and rooting for the Indianapolis Colts—specifically for their head coach, Chuck Pagano.

After a career spent as a coaching assistant with various college and NFL teams, Pagano became the Colts' head coach in 2012. Unfortunately, only three weeks into the regular season, the unthinkable happened: the rookie coach was diagnosed with acute promyelocytic leukemia. Forced to step away from his dream job, Coach Pagano faced weeks of chemotherapy treatments and an uncertain future. He would be sidelined for an indefinite period of time, and his doctors said it was unlikely he'd return during that season. His recovery would depend on how his body reacted to daily treatments, and as expected, the chemo caused severe side effects.

Confined to his hospital room, Pagano nonetheless continued to coach from his bedside, often emailing and texting players as well as members of his coaching staff. Drawing on their Christian faith, he and his wife, Tina, refused to succumb to fear.

During Pagano's treatment and recovery, Bruce Arians, the team's offensive coach and himself a cancer survivor, stepped into the leader's role. The team already faced the daunting challenge of turning around their previous 2–14 record and breaking in a rookie quarterback. With their new coach sidelined, it seemed likely the Colts would endure another uneven year with a losing record.

But something happened as their coach's battle off the field galvanized the team: they began winning, both on and off the field. Despite significant adversity, the Colts finished the regular season with an 11–5 record and won a spot in the playoffs, far exceeding what most experts had predicted. Not surprisingly, perhaps, seven of their eleven victories were come-from-behind wins in the fourth quarter.

In addition to winning game after game as underdogs, the Colts also helped form CHUCKSTRONG, a nonprofit dedicated to raising money for cancer research and treatment. As Pagano's inspiring story caught on, players, cheerleaders, and fans shaved their heads to show their support for the beloved head coach, who had lost his hair during chemo. Millions of dollars were raised as the movement spread across the country and throughout the NFL. What had first appeared to cripple the team became the unifying factor that made them stronger as they inspired so many others battling cancer.

Coach Pagano grew stronger and went on to defeat the cancer that once threatened his life. By the end of the season, he was able to return to the sidelines, and the following season, he went back to his job full time. His rookie year was not what he had expected, but throughout his entire battle, he never allowed himself to be defined by the cancer. He said, "Adversity will always be part of life. . . . Circumstances don't define us or determine who we are; they only reveal who we are."*

I love that last line because it's so true! No matter what happens, you still have choices. No matter how dark, how bleak, how painful your present circumstances, there is hope if you know Jesus Christ. Just ask the apostle Paul.

Sustained by Kindness

Nothing about Paul's journey to Rome went smoothly. As the old saying goes, it was a comedy of errors. Only there was nothing funny about the numerous delays and diversions impeding his progress toward his destination. And remember, Paul had chosen to go to Rome—both to put the matter of his legal status to rest once and for all and, more importantly, to obey God's call compelling him to go there to share the gospel. You'll recall from the previous chapter that this wasn't a pleasure cruise, a three-hour sightseeing tour around the harbor. It was a prison ship! Here's how the beginning of the voyage is described in Acts:

> When it was decided that we would sail for Italy, Paul and some other
> prisoners were handed over to a centurion named Julius, who belonged
> to the Imperial Regiment. We boarded a ship from Adramyttium about
> to sail for ports along the coast of the province of Asia, and we put out
> to sea. Aristarchus, a Macedonian from Thessalonica, was with us.
>
> The next day we landed at Sidon; and Julius, in kindness to Paul,
> allowed him to go to his friends so they might provide for his needs.
> From there we put out to sea again and passed to the lee of Cyprus
> because the winds were against us. When we had sailed across the open

---

* Chuck Pagano, *Sidelined: Overcoming Odds Through Unity, Passion, and Perseverance* (Grand Rapids, MI: Zondervan, 2014), 181.

sea off the coast of Cilicia and Pamphylia, we landed at Myra in Lycia. There the centurion found an Alexandrian ship sailing for Italy and put us on board. We made slow headway for many days and had difficulty arriving off Cnidus. When the wind did not allow us to hold our course, we sailed to the lee of Crete, opposite Salmone. We moved along the coast with difficulty and came to a place called Fair Havens, near the town of Lasea. (27:1–8)

Although it was a prison ship, the beginning of the journey included bright spots, silver linings within the storm clouds forming on Paul's horizon. Julius, the Roman centurion charged with delivering the prisoners, acted kindly toward Paul by allowing him to go ashore in Sidon so he could visit friends who could "provide for his needs." We're not told exactly what those needs were, but I suspect they were as simple as food, water, and a comfortable bed. Paul may have had wounds or injuries that needed dressing as well.

> **Even when we're experiencing trying situations, we still receive small mercies.**

Whatever the provision he received in Sidon, it's important enough to note and reminds us that even when we're experiencing trying situations, we still receive small mercies, such as the opportunity to enjoy some hospitality from friends. Even today, when we're enduring storms, God blesses us with daily bread and small gifts of kindness and convenience. A text or call from a friend, a hug from a loved one, an invitation to share a meal with neighbors, or even a kind word from a stranger can sustain us when our lives feel out of control.

Sometimes it's simply having someone stop and listen to our stories and what's troubling our hearts that helps us get through a bad day.

It's not easy when you're going through a crisis to recognize the gifts coming your way. But as I like to say, an attitude of gratitude is not just a platitude! Focusing on what God provides, even if it's not all you want or think you need, allows you to take your focus off your problems. Gratitude can help restore your perspective and remind you that your circumstances are not as harsh as they seem. You realize others care and are willing to share the burden of what you're facing. You are not alone in your storm.

And when the waters are calm and the sailing smooth, you can look for opportunities to pass on the blessings, giving those around you the same comfort and kindness that sustained you in past struggles. Certainly, praying for others and their needs is important, but don't underestimate showing you care by offering babysitting services for the single mom in your small group, sharing your lunch with a coworker, or leaving an unexpected large tip for the waitress who messed up your order.

Whether we're giving or receiving, kindness always blesses us.

MAKE YOU OR BREAK YOU

Once Paul's ship was on its way again, it didn't take long for problems to start. We're told, "The winds were against us" (Acts 27:4) and that "much time had been lost, and sailing had already become dangerous because by now it was after the Day of Atonement" (verse 9). Knowing that the Jewish holiday traditionally falls late in the year, scholars estimate Paul's voyage took place around the end of September or early October, the beginning of autumn—and of storm season. With winter quickly approaching, it would soon no longer be safe to sail long distances.

The fall-into-winter season was a time of stormy seas, and not much has changed in more than two thousand years. As I write, multiple hurricanes have recently ripped through the Atlantic, leveling islands and coastlines, including my beloved Puerto Rico, where electric power is likely to be out for months. Even with so many of our modern comforts, conveniences, and technological advances, we still experience weather as a mercurial, deadly force.

Paul knew that the storm season was fast approaching and warned, "Men, I can see that our voyage is going to be disastrous and bring great loss to ship and cargo, and to our own lives also" (verse 10). The centurion listened to the boat's captain, however, and they continued on their voyage because they couldn't harbor for the winter where they were. So they sailed on—hoping to reach Phoenix, a harbor in Crete (see verses 11–12) that would offer adequate shelter until better weather in the new year.

Before they could find a safe harbor, Paul's prophetic warning proved true. This is where the story starts to fascinate me, because it's so relevant to similar forces—and similar choices—that you and I face today. Paul's story continues, "Before very long, a wind of hurricane force, called the Northeaster, swept down from the island. *The ship was caught by the storm* and could not head into the wind; *so we gave way to it and were driven along*" (verses 14–15).

In many ways, this is the crux of the story. The ship was caught by the storm, and how did those aboard respond? They gave way to it and were driven along. Is there any better image for how we feel when we're caught off guard and forced to contend with a scary diagnosis, a heartbreaking betrayal, or a lost opportunity? Suddenly life spins out of control—out of *our* control—and we feel like a passenger trapped on a cruise ship during a hurricane.

In these moments it's so tempting to feel like victims and yield to a passive mind-set. When life feels out of control, we often resign to "fate" and brace for the worst, allowing ourselves to be tossed from one painful event to the next. When this happens, we need to recall what Coach Pagano said, that these storms do not control our lives. They don't define us or change who we are. No, they only reveal who we *really* are and what has been driving us all along.

The longer I follow Jesus, the more I'm convinced that Christianity is less about what we drive and more about what drives us. The storms always come; it's simply the consequence of living in a world where men and women can choose freely whether to serve God or their own desires. And when those storms come, they strip away the veneer of polite pretense and the facade of cultural faith. Pretending to know God when the wind howls and the waves crash around you won't cut it. That's when you discover the depth of your faith. That's when you discover what you're made of.

DRAMA OR DESTINY

Think about the kind of week you're having. Day to day, as you go from home to work or school and back home again, what drives you? What gets you out of bed in the morning and causes you to greet the day with joy instead of dread?

The Japanese have a word, *ikigai,* that captures this sense of drive we all have inside us. Roughly translated as "the happiness of constant busyness," *ikigai* reflects your awareness of your life's purpose as well as how you go about fulfilling it.

Do you know your God-given purpose? Is it really what drives you most days? Or is it something else—making more money, pleasing your boss, achieving that promotion? We are all driven people, but when push comes to shove, not all of us are driven by our faith. When the storm begins to churn around you, when the police call in the middle of the night or the accidental email gets sent, when the account is overdrawn or the friendly smile becomes seductive, your faith will be tested.

In those moments you will be driven either by drama or by destiny.

When the storm breaks in your life, you will be driven by either

- the past or the future
- the pathetic or the prophetic
- problems or promises

41

- nightmares or dreams
- the flesh or the Spirit
- Google searches or godly churches
- the drama of the storm or God's destiny for your life

Notice that *destiny* and *destination* share the same origin, coming from the Latin *destinare,* meaning to bind or intend or determine.* Basically, they both refer to the direction of your life and how you're traveling along the way. For instance, are you driven by the praise of others? Or by the criticism of others? Neither should influence your life's direction or how you respond in a storm. If others' praise didn't make you, their criticism cannot break you!

Never let your problems drive your direction. Don't let your crisis become your compass. We have too many Christians who continue to be driven by personal drama rather than godly destiny. Too many who spend more time reacting to what comes from hell rather than what comes from heaven and to what people say about them rather than what God did for them.

Do not be driven by what you see; be driven by what God said.

Do not be driven by past mistakes; be driven by future miracles.

Do not be driven by feelings; be driven by faith.

Do not be driven by being a victim; be driven by being victorious.

Let all you are and all you do be driven by the Spirit of God, "for those who are led by the Spirit of God are the children of God" (Romans 8:14).

In Christ, nothing in your battered past has the power to hold back your beautiful future!

CHOOSE IT OR LOSE IT

No matter how harsh the storm or how devastating its impact, you always get to choose how you respond. You may certainly feel that you have no choice and

---

* Latdict, s.v. *"destino, destinare, destinavi, destinatus,"* http://latin-dictionary.net/definition/17089/destino
-destinare-destinavi-destinatus.

that you're powerless as the storm tosses you back and forth and determines where you end up. But that's not true! You always have choices about how you respond to the storm.

And when you choose to trust God and keep going by faith, you know that the storm has no power over you. It may toss you around and leave you a little seasick, but ultimately God is more powerful than any storm. I mean *any storm*! Even storms such as cancer, divorce, abuse, bankruptcy, addiction, and adultery.

Think of the very worst thing you can imagine in your life and realize right now that even in the midst of crippling pain from a shattered heart, you would still have a choice. Like the choice Job faced after experiencing unthinkable losses and Paul was given on a ragtag prison ship, you can choose fear or you can choose faith.

If you choose fear, you'll allow the storm to drive your life. But if you choose faith, your destiny will be greater than the drama.

Your miracle will redeem the mistake.

Your dream will put an end to the nightmare.

And God's blessing will overtake your brokenness.

The storm does not make you, and it will break you only if you let it. The storm exposes who you really are and what you really believe. God not only wants you to survive; he wants you to thrive!

I learned this lesson early in life. As I mentioned, I grew up in a very healthy, loving Christian family, but that didn't mean my life was easy—far from it. As a quiet, studious, science fiction–loving Puerto Rican nerd, I faced more than my fair share of prejudice, bullying, and abuse—not just from peers but from adults as well.

I'll never forget sitting in the guidance counselor's office my freshman year in high school in the Lehigh Valley area between Philadelphia and Allentown, where I grew up. The purpose of our meeting was to discuss my vocational direction and the courses I should and hoped to take the following semester.

Since our school was located in a mostly working-class area, students were placed into one of two groups pretty quickly: either you were smart enough and your parents wealthy enough that you were headed to college and a professional career, or you were not smart enough or your family wealthy enough for college, so you got a basic education and learned a trade.

"So what do you want to do when you get out of school, Sam?" the guidance counselor asked. "What kind of job are you thinking about?"

"Well," I said nervously, "I'm really into computers and hoping to study computer engineering at one of the state universities."

"No, Sam, I'm not kidding," she said, genuinely agitated. "Your kind doesn't go to college. You can work either construction or landscaping or get some other kind of service job."

That hurt.

Even though I had good grades that put me at the top of my class and I tested high on all aptitude and intelligence tests, this woman's prejudice sent gale-force winds over the dream of a shy fifteen-year-old. And the worst part about it was that she seemed totally oblivious to the devastating power of her words. I knew two things when I left her office that day. First, whatever I did later in life, I was going to make sure it wasn't one of the three options she'd mentioned. While there's nothing wrong with any of these jobs and the hard-working people who do them, I desired a different path. Second, I decided to work harder than ever to graduate at the top of my class. So being salutatorian when graduation day came gave me deep satisfaction!

CHOOSE FOR GOOD

I was most fortunate. Having a loving, supportive family and being blessed with the intelligence to see beyond this woman's ignorance allowed me to escape a storm that could have stunted my growth permanently. Maybe you had a similar experience at an early age, when someone tried to hold you back and prevent you from becoming the person God created you to be. Maybe you're still carrying around the scars from someone's wounds to your confidence and creativity. Perhaps you're still hiding from a storm that ended a long time ago.

My friend, if you look to Christ, you will know it's time to come out of hiding into the glorious adventure of your joyful purpose. The storms of life will always come, but they have no power to determine your destination. God alone is in charge of where you're going and how you're going to get there. Paul wrote, "And we know that in all things God works for the good of those who love him, who have been called according to his purpose" (Romans 8:28).

Notice that Paul said *all* things—not some things or a few things but all things. God can redeem even the worst storms you have been through or are going through right now. You can't see a way out, but he has already prepared a way. All you have to do is take the next step of faith and keep going. You have a choice about how you will react when storms come. You may not feel like keeping going, and the choice probably won't appear logical or even rational, but the decision is yours.

You can choose faith and trust that the One who made you will be faithful as he has promised. You can choose to keep moving in his direction instead of allowing the currents of circumstance to divert you from your destination. No matter what choices you've made in the past, whether years ago or just yesterday, God loves you and will see you safely through any storm.

Don't be driven by drama, diversion, or distraction. Be driven by the Spirit of God within you!

Shake Free . . . from Circumstantial Storms

As you ask God to empower you to weather the storms of life, use the following questions to help you reflect. Invite his Spirit to speak to your heart and strengthen your resolve so that you will continue to trust in him rather than be rattled by circumstances.

1. What storms are you weathering right now? How are you coping with these challenging circumstances?

2. Do you tend to be more reactive or proactive? In other words, how much control do you usually try to exert over the events in your everyday life? Do you wait and see what happens and then act? Or do you take deliberate actions regardless of what your day holds?

3. What drives you each day as you journey toward the divine destination God has for you? How can you surrender more fully and yield all areas of your life to the Holy Spirit?

Lord, I often feel powerless and frustrated in light of circumstances beyond my control. When the storms rage around me, I get discouraged and begin to allow fear and worry to consume me. During these tumultuous times, keep me safe in the palm of your hand, God. You are so powerful and can see me through whatever storms I may be facing now or in the future. I have nothing to fear because I know you are with me. You have equipped me and empowered me to withstand the wind and rain and to trust that I will see not only the sun again but also the beautiful reminder of your promises, the rainbow. Thank you for loving me so much and giving me a destiny that no storm can destroy or divert me from fulfilling. Amen.

4

No Longer Anchored in Fear

Feed your fears, and your faith will starve.
Feed your faith, and your fears will.

—Max Lucado, *Fearless*

'll never forget the first time I preached. I can still remember the sheer terror gripping my body as I smiled nervously, prayed silently, and stepped into the pulpit at the church near Allentown, Pennsylvania, where I was a youth pastor. I wasn't much older than the kids I was leading, and when our senior pastor asked me to fill in for him, I was honored by his confidence in giving me the opportunity. My excitement, however, quickly melted into the fear of speaking in front of so many people.

Preparing my sermon all week, I didn't have butterflies inside me but rather a minefield of what-ifs waiting to explode in front of our entire congregation. What if my mouth got so dry I couldn't swallow? What if I took a drink of water for my dry mouth and choked—literally? What if I lost my place in my outline and couldn't remember what I'd just said? What if I went too fast and no one could understand me? What if the mic quit working for some reason?

What if, what if, what if?

Some moments I even considered backing out. But I knew if I didn't preach that day, I would probably never be asked to preach again. I'm not sure that's true, but it felt true at the time. Faced with not just public speaking but also preaching, I began to question my calling. Maybe I wasn't cut out for being a pastor after all. Maybe I should've stuck with computer engineering. Maybe I should have settled for something less demanding, some job that didn't require me to stand up in front of hundreds (and later, *thousands*) of people and risk revealing myself—and my lack of confidence.

Maybe, maybe, maybe.

Knowing I was not the only one afraid of public speaking brought me no comfort. Research continues to confirm that many people are more afraid of public speaking than they are of heights, jumping out of planes, or even dying. As American author and humorist Mark Twain once said, "There are two types of speakers: Those who get nervous and those who are liars."*

Fortunately, I got through that first sermon without anyone falling asleep in the pew or dashing out the door. I honestly don't remember what I preached on that Sunday morning, only that shortly after I opened my mouth and started talking, something happened. Looking back now, I would explain it as God's Spirit speaking through me, using me as his vessel to deliver the message he had placed on my heart.

Somehow, to my amazement, that morning I suddenly felt more determined to ignore my fears and do what I knew God wanted me to do. My voice was calmer, louder, and more passionate than ever before. And I think everyone in our sanctuary that day was as surprised as I was. They knew me as this quiet, polite, enthusiastic youth pastor, but there I was proclaiming God's Word at the top of my lungs like a man set on fire!

Now when people hear me preach, they can't imagine I was ever that quiet, shy young man who considered leaving ministry because of his fears. They as-

---

* Mark Twain, quoted in Jerry Weissman, "Another Humorous View on the Fear of Public Speaking," *Forbes*, June 17, 2014, www.forbes.com/sites/jerryweissman/2014/06/17/another-humorous-view-on-the-fear-of -public-speaking/#49bf72016708.

sume that I never get nervous anymore or that I never battle anxiety or fears, but I do. I'm just as human as anyone else, and I still have days when it seems so much easier to settle for being comfortable and quiet rather than stepping forward in faith toward what God has for me. I suspect we all battle such moments when we're tempted to lower our anchors when faced with life's storms and resign ourselves to defeat.

The crewmen on Paul's voyage reacted this way. They assumed there was no way to survive such a brutal, relentless storm. They did what seemed logical based on their fears. But anchoring ourselves in our fears never helps us reach our destinations.

A PERFECT STORM

In the last chapter we left Paul and his fellow shipmates rocking and rolling along the coast of Crete in what must have been a perfect storm, the term scientists and meteorologists use for the confluence of atmospheric and oceanic conditions that generate the most powerful storms imaginable. With hurricane-force winds that easily exceed 150 miles per hour and waves the size of small buildings, these storms send sailors scrambling for a safe harbor and coastal residents evacuating to higher ground.

Maybe you've read Sebastian Junger's best-selling book *The Perfect Storm* or seen the film version. Both describe the true tale of the fishing ship *Andrea Gail,* which vanished, leaving no survivors, during an epic, once-in-a-century storm off the coast of Massachusetts in 1991. I mention this tragic tale because I continue to think of that movie whenever I read this account of Paul's plight: "Before very long, a wind of hurricane force, called the Northeaster, swept down from the island" (Acts 27:14).

You don't need to have set foot on a boat to experience one of life's perfect storms. Sometimes we experience one huge, devastating loss, only to have it compounded and complicated by another and then another. Maybe you know someone who lost his job, which led to depression and a recurrence of alcohol and substance abuse. Caught in the downward spiral of addiction, he lost control of his finances until he was forced to declare bankruptcy. Then because he was unwilling to seek help, his wife left them and took their children. One harsh event is all it sometimes takes to topple dominoes of destruction across the path of one's divine destiny.

Perhaps you suffered broken bones and debilitating injuries in a car accident that has left you combating chronic pain on a daily basis. There you were, driving to work, when a careless driver T-boned your car. Now, after numerous surgeries and weeks of rehabilitation, you're discovering that your life will never be the same. You can no longer do your job or enjoy the quality of life you knew prior to the accident. Every day you wake up and feel as if you're trapped in a perpetual storm of rage, pain, and fear.

Or maybe it's simply the possibility of facing a perfect storm that keeps you on edge and constantly scanning the horizon for the next circumstantial crisis or personal disaster. More and more, I encounter people who struggle with this mind-set of anxiety and worry, battling their own personal what-ifs and maybes as they wait for the other shoe to drop.

With so much turmoil in our world today, it's no wonder that PTSD—posttraumatic stress disorder, a condition primarily diagnosed in veterans and other survivors of intense violence or trauma—has become a mainstream term.

From teens enduring cyberbullies to soccer moms struggling to juggle the demands of their families, from recent college grads searching fruitlessly for jobs in their fields to corporate managers forced to change careers, most everyone in our world's developed countries battles stress on a daily basis. Even simple things like business travel or going to the mall now seem tinged with the possibility of terrorist activity. Allowed to run unfettered, our fears can quickly grow like a cancer and spread into all areas of our thoughts, actions, and daily lives.

But only if we let them.

The beautiful thing about faith is that it secures us to God, a loving Father, who is bigger, more powerful, and more sovereign than any force on earth. Our faith is the only anchor we need when a perfect storm hits. Any other will just leave us more fearful.

FUELED BY FEAR

Many times the choice to drop anchor in the middle of a storm makes total sense from a human, logical perspective. This seems to be the reason the sailors on Paul's ship chose this option after struggling against their raging north-easter. We read,

> As we passed to the lee of a small island called Cauda, we were hardly
> able to make the lifeboat secure, so the men hoisted it aboard. Then they
> passed ropes under the ship itself to hold it together. Because they were
> afraid they would run aground on the sandbars of Syrtis, they lowered
> the sea anchor and let the ship be driven along. (Acts 27:16–17)

This makes sense, doesn't it? They anticipated needing the ship's lifeboat, so they made sure one of those giant waves didn't rip it off the side of the ship, where it was apparently tied. The crew couldn't secure the lifeboat well enough to guarantee it would stay in place, so they hoisted it onto their ship.

Then notice this next detail: "They passed ropes under the ship itself to hold it together." The ship was literally coming apart at the seams! The pegs or nails holding the vessel together could not withstand the battering force of the wind and waves. All the sailors could do was tie their ship together with ropes.

Then, finally, they did the only other thing that seemed logical in their predicament: they lowered anchor.

When I asked a friend who likes to sail why the crew on Paul's ship would do this, my friend explained that in most storms, lowering anchor was a traditional strategy to keep the boat from being tossed off course. By tossing anchor and staying put, sailors can usually wait out a storm and then, after the seas become calm again, resume the course they were sailing.

I don't have a problem with the sailors on Paul's ship taking such measures. No, my problem is that they were taking this action *motivated by fear*. After ignoring Paul's warning about setting sail (see verses 9–10), the captain and crew gave in to their fear and allowed it to drive their decisions. Please understand that I don't fault them for being afraid, especially considering I get seasick in the bathtub! Our feelings aren't necessarily controllable; it's how we respond to our feelings that makes all the difference. In this case, they were far from Rome, far from their destination, far from their appointment, but *because of fear* they lowered their anchor. The big problem here is simply allowing fear to determine the course of action.

Fear prompted them to lower the anchor.

Fear drove them to get stuck in the storm.

Fear consumed their ability to see beyond the present storm.

How we respond to our feelings makes all the difference.

When my kids were little, they loved corny jokes, and one of their favorites was "What do you call a scared piece of string when it gets tied up? Afraid knot!" As silly as it is, this joke always reminds me that when we allow fear to tie us up in knots, we end up unraveling. Giving in to fear always leaves us feeling exhausted, depleted, frayed, and frustrated.

So we do what we know to do: we toss our anchor. We get to the end of our ropes and we tie knots and try to hang on, but eventually we get tired and our hands cramp and the ropes fray and we try to tie more knots, only to discover that we can't hold on by our own power. We simply can't do it. An old cliché tells us to "let go and let God," and in the middle of a storm, its wisdom holds true. So often we can't discover what God wants to give us because we're clinging so tightly to our own anchors.

STUCK IN THE STORM

How do you handle your fear in the midst of a storm? When have you allowed your fears to determine your actions? As you think through your response, I would also encourage you to identify the chronic fears you tend to face on a daily basis. Are you afraid of failure, of rejection, of being abandoned? Do you worry about not being accepted, not being loved, being betrayed? We all struggle with fear, but our Enemy tends to exploit our personalities and circumstances to create personal fears tailored just for us.

Like a virus weakening the strength of our bodies, fear depletes our faith. Fear is the enemy of faith, causing us to drop anchor and stop short of reaching our God-given destinations.

Fear made Adam and Eve hide from God in the garden (see Genesis 3:8).

Fear prompted Elijah to hide from Jezebel (see 1 Kings 19:1–3).

Fear caused Peter to sink in the lake, and it eroded his faith to the point that he denied Christ three times (see Matthew 14:29–30; 26:69–75).

At one time or another, we all must confront our worst fears, both within and without. Fear of looking through windows, of what we see in the outside world. Fear of looking in mirrors, of what we see within ourselves. But there's another way to see our lives and everything around us: through the lens of faith. We cannot see clearly with our limited human vision. But when we trust

God for where we're going and how we'll get there, we are no longer consumed by our fears. We're told, "God has not given us a spirit of fear but of power and of love and of a sound mind" (2 Timothy 1:7, NKJV).

But the sailors feared and gave in to the storm's destructive power.

They feared not making it.

They feared failure.

They feared death.

So they dropped the anchor and resigned themselves to being torn apart by the storm. You know what I'm talking about. Because of fear, because of the spiritual, relational or financial storm, you dropped your faith, quit praising God, let go of holiness, surrendered your dream, and lost sight of your divinely designated destination. You gave up on getting to Rome because the storm was too fierce and your fear too great.

Maybe you're still there right now, feeling stuck in the proverbial backwaters of life, because you continue to focus more on the storm than on the destination.

You are stuck because of what you do to yourself.

You are stuck because of what others did to you.

You are stuck because of what others said about you.

You're not moving or growing. You're not truly living, only going through the motions. Everything feels stuck in place—your joy, your faith, your dream, your calling. Your integrity is stuck. Your finances are stuck. You're at a plateau of passivity because of all the fears swirling around you. You're not getting anywhere because you've lowered your anchor. You continue to rely on your own power and what should work, even though you know it can't work the way things are. You're stuck in the storm. But you don't have to stay that way!

If you want to get unstuck, you need a new sail.

You need to replace fear with faith.

You need the power of perfect love.

THE POWER OF PERFECT LOVE

If you want to get unstuck, God will help you raise your anchor and give you higher ground—a Solid Rock to cling to when the storms of life blow. In his Word, God reveals the remedy for being stuck in fear: *"Perfect love expels all fear"* (1 John 4:18, NLT). Who is the source of perfect love? Only our holy God! He first loved us so that we can know what it means to love. By his example we learn to love him in return. We learn to love ourselves in healthy, godly ways. We learn to love others the way Jesus loved others. And we learn to expel fear.

Your faith will no longer be stuck in place. It will be active and dynamic, growing and maturing to produce the fruit of the Spirit. You will experience a satisfaction you've never known as you live out your God-given purpose and serve others with your unique talents and through divinely appointed opportunities. Your hunger to know God and your thirst for Living Water will be satisfied each day as you grow closer to Christ and your faith strengthens.

Your relationships will not be stuck anymore. You will experience the ability to forgive others and ask for their forgiveness. You will demonstrate God's grace and mercy and reflect his glory in all that you say and do. You will love and serve with gladness because of the joy of the Lord bubbling up inside you.

Your future will not be stuck. God has a hope and a purpose for you, and it's no accident that you are exactly where you are. No matter how bleak or barren your circumstances, God can help you pull up your anchor and get you moving through this storm. He will be faithful to keep his promises and make sure you get where you're supposed to be. He will guide you to Rome no matter where you're located now.

But you have to choose the power of love and the strength of faith over the cancer of fear attacking you with each setback, disappointment, or obstacle. You have to exercise the free will God has given you and refuse to give in to fear. I don't care how afraid you feel—you are not your feelings! You have a mind and a heart and a spirit and a body that are not defined by how you feel. No matter how horrendous your storm or how heavy your anchor, God's love can cast out your fear.

If you want to stay stuck in your past, stuck in your misery, stuck in your pain, stuck in your sin, then this solution is not for you. But if you're ready to get unstuck and start moving again, ready to step into your destiny and stop trying so hard in your own power, ready to stop settling and start trusting, then you don't have to be locked in fear when the storms rage around you.

Paul wrote, "I press toward the goal for the prize of the upward call of God in Christ Jesus" (Philippians 3:14, NKJV). God is not looking for those halted by fear but for those driven by faith. It's not that he's unwilling to help those who are stuck in fear—just the opposite! He simply cannot help those who cling to fear instead of entering the warm, rescuing embrace of their Father who loves them so much that he sent his only Son to die for them.

Don't settle for less than God's best in your life. If past wounds, present circumstances, or future worries have caused you to get stuck in a storm, it's time to make your move. Allow the Lord who saves you to empower you with the perfect love that casts out all fear. His love is the lifeline that shatters your fear once and for all!

SHAKE FREE . . . FROM FEAR

Use the following questions to help you reflect on how God's perfect love casts out the fear in your life.

1. What's your worst fear right now? What are you most terrified of losing? How does your fear motivate your daily actions and behaviors?

2. What are some temporary anchors you've relied on to help you face storms in the past? How did these work out for you? Which strategies of self-reliance continue to be part of your default setting when something hard happens?

3. What would your life look like if you replaced that fear you're carrying around with God's perfect love? What would be the biggest difference in your attitude? In your habits and lifestyle?

_____

Lord, you know the fears I combat on a daily basis. I'm exhausted by them and refuse to live my life ruled by them any longer. Forgive me for not trusting you with my whole heart in all areas of my life. Thank you for your perfect love that has the power to expel all my fears. Please help me replace my fears with faith that I can do all things through you and the power of your Holy Spirit. I will no longer be stuck but will follow you to the destination I know you have for me. Amen.

5

You Will Make It Even Without Your Ship

We never understand how little we need
in this world until we know the loss of it.

—J. M. Barrie, *Margaret Ogilvy*

had never felt so lost in my entire life. While visiting friends in Denver, I decided to check out Rocky Mountain National Park and do a little hiking. It was early summer and the weather seemed perfect—cool and sunny. I enjoy running and usually work out on tracks, urban sidewalks, and indoor treadmills, so the thought of trail running in the gorgeous splendor of the snowcapped Rockies was more than enough motivation to lace up my Nikes. I usually like having a running partner, but that day I was alone and grateful for some solitude after a busy travel season.

Well aware of the impact the high altitude was having on my lungs, I planned to just take it easy, soak up some sun, and breathe in the crisp, clean mountain air. I had chosen a trail that was fairly remote, away from the summer tourists, and wore a running belt with a small water bottle and a pouch for an energy bar.

My run began with that glorious feeling one has when surrounded by the natural beauty of God's creation. After encountering a couple of hikers, I set a gentle pace and followed the trail into deeply wooded terrain.

Sunlight filtered through dense evergreens as the trail slowly ascended. After a half hour, I reached an overlook and couldn't believe the grandeur of the mountains rising in beautiful, jagged peaks around me. Sipping my water, I noticed the air was cooler, as the sun had begun playing hide-and-seek behind a column of clouds forming overhead. It wasn't supposed to rain, but I had been warned about the summer thunderstorms that often appear out of nowhere. It wasn't the rain that concerned me but rather the intense lightning that usually accompanies these impromptu storms.

Making a mental note to keep an eye on the clouds, I resumed my run and didn't see a soul, just a hawk—or was it an eagle?—soaring high above the tree line on the mountain facing me. When I finally reached the lookout I had chosen for my turnaround, it was almost noon, so I paused to eat my energy bar and have some more water. Grateful to absorb the Creator's handiwork in such a setting, I breathed deeply and thanked God for the tranquility and solitude of this restorative time.

That's when the first cold raindrop splattered my face.

Gray clouds now blanketed much of the sky, smothering all hints of the sun I'd been enjoying only moments ago. The wind picked up as more rain fell, and to find shelter, I dashed beneath a grove of aspen trees just off the trail. Then a jagged thread of white-hot electric current flickered across the heavens, and the sky rumbled with a mighty boom.

This was not good.

With only my running shorts and T-shirt, I was already starting to shiver. And while I hoped this might be one of those little storms just passing through, the clouds only grew denser, darker, and angrier. Right then another lightning bolt flared, striking the rocky ground only fifty yards away, which finalized my decision to run for it.

Puddles formed atop the dry, dusty ground before streaming down the natural line of descent made by the trail; flash floods were another problem in the high-country summers. As I tried to run, sheets of rain stung my face with wet slaps of cold water, and thunder ricocheted along the mountaintops as more lightning blazed overhead.

The rain fell so hard I had trouble seeing more than a foot or two in front of me. Following the trail more from memory than by sight, I turned a corner to what I thought should be a switchback, only to come up against a giant boulder. Making a U-turn, I turned back and couldn't see the trail, only the path I'd just made in the mud. All I could see was a rocky hillside studded with more boulders. Somehow I had gone off trail. (As if this situation could get any worse!)

I'll admit it—for about thirty seconds there, I panicked. Panting in the cold mountain rain, soaking wet and shivering, my nice white running shoes painted muddy brown, I had no idea where I was or how long this storm was going to last. I had no water, no food, no compass, and no clue! As I said, I'd never felt more lost in my life.

Stumbling on in the storm, I came to a horseshoe-shaped collection of boulders that formed a kind of natural shelter, almost like a cave, so I decided to stop and try to get my bearings. All around me the indigo sky crackled with lightning, like an enormous bowl shattering along its edges. I caught my breath, said a prayer, and wondered how I would find my way back. If nothing else, I could keep going downhill and orient myself by the westward descent of the sun—assuming the storm ever stopped and the clouds cleared.

After what seemed like hours but was probably only fifteen minutes, the bruised clouds became more luminous as the downpour relented, fading to a steady shower. Thunder and lightning subsided as small shafts of sunlight began penetrating the cloud cover. The rain dissolved into a fine mist as I began slipping and sliding downhill, thrilled to discover the trail sloping about two hundred yards away from my little shelter. From there it took me less than an hour to make my way back to the trailhead. Although I was a muddy, soggy mess when I got there, I was relieved and exhilarated.

GOING OVERBOARD

When I think about the hurricane-force northeaster Paul endured on his voyage to Rome, I remember my little experience of a few hours in the Rockies and wonder how I would have endured his storm that lasted for weeks.

As the storm raged on and on, the crew of Paul's ship grasped the idea that desperate times call for desperate measures. They had already brought the lifeboat onto the deck of the ship and thrown anchor overboard to help steady the ship and keep it on course. But sheets of rain continued to clash with gigantic waves, pounding the ship with its 276 men onboard (see Acts 27:37) as if it were a toy boat stuck beneath Niagara Falls. So they did the unthinkable on a cargo ship in a last-ditch effort to lighten its weight: they began throwing *everything* overboard! Scripture describes the experience like this:

> We took such a violent battering from the storm that the next day they
> began to throw the cargo overboard. On the third day, they threw the
> ship's tackle overboard with their own hands. When neither sun nor
> stars appeared for many days and the storm continued raging, we finally
> gave up all hope of being saved. (verses 18–20)

Caught in the hurricane's rain-filled winds and the giant swells of the churning sea, the boat risked flooding, so the crew threw not only the ship's cargo overboard but the tackle as well! For a cargo ship's crew to toss its cargo, they might as well have been throwing money away. Then to throw the tackle overboard? That was suicide! The nautical tackle consisted of the ropes, pulleys, and chains used to hoist sails and guide the ship, along with various tools needed for nautical maintenance. So tossing the ship's tackle would be like throwing your car's steering wheel out the window on a road trip! Such last-resort measures highlight the sheer desperation these men felt.

Can you imagine being soaked to the bone without any idea whether it was night or day, with no end in sight? These passengers and crew had to be wondering, *Will this storm ever end?* When caught in the middle of a crisis, most of us feel the same way. Our personal storms often feel all consuming, and we lose our sense of perspective. We start to go overboard in our attempts to regain control of our situations. It seems as if the pain of our grief, the physical suffering of our injuries, or the crushing emotional burden of our financial debt will never end.

> **Our personal storms often feel all consuming, and we lose our sense of perspective.**

When a betrayal occurs or your child disappears into addiction, you may feel as though a trapdoor has opened beneath your feet. You begin free-falling with no idea where, how, when, or even if you'll land and ever be back on your feet again. Others may offer to help and extend their hands to hold you, but no one feels strong enough.

No one, that is, except God.

This is what Paul reminded his panicked fellow passengers during their seemingly never-ending storm. We read in verses 21–22,

> After they had gone a long time without food, Paul stood up before them and said: "Men, you should have taken my advice not to sail from Crete; then you would have spared yourselves this damage and loss. But now I urge you to keep up your courage, because not one of you will be lost; only the ship will be destroyed."

Now, before you think Paul was basically just rubbing their faces in a big "I told you so," consider his motive. As they frantically tried to save the ship—and their own lives—it really was not the best time to remind the others that he was right. I suspect he was reminding the others that *God* was right—God had inspired Paul to warn the sailors previously. Paul's recalling to those on-board that God's prophetic message had proven true was important because Paul was about to deliver another prediction: not one life would be lost, even though the ship would be destroyed.

LIFE PRESERVER

Paul's newest message had to sound absurd to the other passengers, considering their situation. How in the world could he predict that all of them would live, when all signs pointed to just the opposite? And how were they going to survive without the ship, which he said would be destroyed? Perhaps some thought Paul was crazy—after all, he was just a lowly prisoner. Or maybe they just thought him naive and inexperienced about sailing. Yet maybe, just maybe, a few of the crew and other passengers believed Paul and prayed he was right even though they couldn't fathom how.

Paul knew that what God places in us is always greater than anything hell places in front of us. The same remains true for us today. Your destiny is not based on what's in front of you. Your destiny is based on who's inside you. Remember: the storm does not make you; the storm exposes who you really are.

This message has never been timelier than in the twenty-first century. As I am writing this, our nation is weathering a mighty storm—more than one, in fact. People living in Houston and along the Gulf Coast, along with those in Florida and especially Puerto Rico, continue to recover from not one but three consecutive hurricanes that struck in less than a month. As if natural disasters weren't enough, the worst mass shooting in our country's history occurred in

Las Vegas, leaving more than fifty dead and more than five hundred injured. Next came the deadliest American church shooting ever, in Texas.

In the midst of such devastation, it can be tempting to lose hope and give up. You simply cannot imagine rebuilding yet again and creating a home, knowing that it, too, might be leveled by a storm. You can't see how you can keep going after losing a loved one or suffering a permanent debilitating injury. You're exhausted and there's nothing to look forward to, no relief from the relentless emotions and crippling circumstances.

It's a good thing we are not people without hope. "In this world you will have trouble," Jesus said. "But take heart! I have overcome the world" (John 16:33). With God's Spirit dwelling in us, we may face the same tragedies and heartaches as anyone else, but the promise of God's presence makes an enormous difference—an eternal difference.

Even during dark days and perilous nights, we have the Light of the World. We have what matters most: our relationship with God. Even if we lose our ship, we won't drown. Why? Because God said so! Through Paul's prophecy he told the people onboard the ship that they would all be saved, and they were. The timeless truth of God's Word continues to reveal his loving promises to us today.

Even when the worst-case scenario becomes our reality, we must not despair. Yes, sometimes the unthinkable happens. Storms wipe out entire island cities and villages. A madman yields to evil and shoots hundreds of innocent people. A raging atheist executes people in a Sunday worship service. Terrible, painful events happen. Storms will always come. Sometimes we even lose our ship, but with or without the ship, God says we will make it. His Word is our life preserver.

What we have lost will not hinder what we will conquer!

Just think about how far God has brought you. It's no accident that you're reading these words right now. Reflect for a moment on what and who you may have lost in your life so far: relationships, homes, jobs, loved ones, your health.

Yet here you are. You're still here and you're still longing to hope, to believe, to dare, and to trust the One who controls your destiny.

> **Just think about how far God has brought you.**

You're alive.

You did not drown.

You did not perish.

And why are you here? Because you had faith! Because God did not bring you this far to let you die without seeing the promise. You are here not because of your personality, intellectual acumen, financial wherewithal, or even your spiritual fortitude. You are here because the Spirit who raised Jesus from the dead is the same Spirit who lives in you (see Romans 8:11). That's a promise from the living God.

You are alive for a reason.

The storms of life have not claimed you.

He who is in you is stronger than anything you face in the world.

Anything.

LOST AND FOUND

No matter how bleak your situation may seem—and I do not say this lightly—it's time to stop moaning about that ship you lost. Stop asking God to restore your past. Stop clinging to what you should have thrown overboard a long time ago.

God is not interested in renovating your past; God is interested in releasing your future.

We're told, "I consider everything a loss because of the surpassing worth of knowing Christ Jesus my Lord, for whose sake I have lost all things. I consider them garbage, that I may gain Christ" (Philippians 3:8). You have all you need in Jesus Christ. It may not feel that way, and it may not be what you want, but you have all you need. You will make it through whatever storm you're in now or any you might face in the future.

I told you my story about getting lost in the storm during my run in the Rockies not because it's the worst thing I've ever been through—far from it! But in the moment, during that hour or so when I was shivering and dazed and lost in unfamiliar terrain, it *felt* like the worst thing possible. Telling you about it now, however, only makes me smile at how intensely I felt lost. No matter how scary it felt at the time, now it's nothing more than a memorable story. I can even laugh about it.

And while you may never be able to laugh about what you're grieving right now or the loss you may be suffering, you can be comforted. You can know the peace that passes all human understanding. God has promised to be with us and never abandon us. His presence is his promise.

You are not alone, no matter how lonely you might feel.

You are loved, no matter how unlovable you may feel.

You are forgiven, no matter how ashamed you might feel.

You are not lost; you are found and lovingly carried by the Good Shepherd.

There is no storm that can rob you of your heavenly shelter. What you've lost cannot compare to where you are going! And what you've lost cannot compare to what God is sending your way, the destination he has waiting for you, the Rome that's just ahead beyond the storm.

We see this pattern of God's possibility revealed in what we see as impossible. Jesus said, "With man this is impossible, but with God all things are possible" (Matthew 19:26). Moses crossing the Red Sea, Joshua marching around the Jericho wall, Paul sailing to Rome. It's relying on God when we come up against life's obstacles that determines the outcome. In Christ, we are more than conquerors—we are unstoppable!

Even without that ship.

Even without that person you thought was going to be with you on the way.

Even without that job you worked so hard to attain.

Even without that promotion that went to a less qualified candidate.

Even without that home you sacrificed to purchase.

Even without that income stream you were counting on.

Even without that retirement fund you lost in the recession.

Even without that relationship you built your world around.

No matter what you've lost, my friend, you are still going to make it!

It's not Sam Rodriguez or even the apostle Paul who says so. Your God says so!

SHAKE FREE . . . FROM LOSS

Use the following questions as you consider how to move on from what you've lost in order to find all that God has for you.

1. What is the greatest loss you're carrying with you right now? How long have you been carrying it? How have you handled the pain of this past storm that continues to linger in your life?

2. What have you lost that you've allowed to come between you and God? What keeps you from trusting that he can restore and redeem even your most painful wounds and losses? Are you willing to trust him with this loss now?

3. God tells us,

Don't be afraid, for I am with you.
    Don't be discouraged, for I am your God.
I will strengthen you and help you.
    I will hold you up with my victorious right hand.
        (Isaiah 41:10, NLT)

What fears do you need to surrender to God as you claim the power of his promise in this verse?

———————————————————

Heavenly Father, life is so painful sometimes. Even when my immediate circumstances are okay, my heart still hurts for all the people I know—and those I don't know—who are suffering and hurting. Too often I allow my past losses to fuel new fears. But I want to trust you, Lord, and claim your promises for my life and my future. No matter what I've lost or may lose, I know that if I have you, I have all I need. And you have promised never to leave me. Thank you, God, for being with me and giving me the power to endure any storm life throws at me. Thank you for all you want to give me when I let go of past losses. Amen.

6

Everyone on Your Ship Will Survive

Blessed is the influence of one true,
loving human soul on another.

—George Eliot

P astor Sam!" a male voice said. "You don't remember me, but I sure remember you!" The speaker had recently friended me on Facebook, asking whether I was the Sam Rodriguez who had served as youth minister
at a church near Allentown, Pennsylvania, back in the nineties. At first I wasn't
able to place the man's name, but after studying his face in the photos on his
profile, I recognized him as one of the members of the church youth group
where I'd pastored. I recalled him as an angry, troubled teen who attended only
sporadically and rarely engaged with me and the rest of our team.

I remembered that his family hadn't attended our church and he'd apparently come to the youth group with friends. Withdrawn and sullen, he made it
clear that he didn't believe much of anything I had to say. I couldn't imagine
why he wanted to contact me nearly twenty years later, but I responded to his
friend request and told him I remembered him.

We then exchanged emails, and this man (I'll call him Mike) asked whether
we could schedule a call. I gave him my number, and we arranged a time to
talk, but the more I thought about it, the more worried I became. What if

Mike blamed me for not pushing through his defenses back then and doing a better job of connecting? What if I had somehow given him a negative impression of who God is and what the gospel is all about? Whatever Mike wanted, I was about to find out.

"Mike," I said, "how in the world are you, brother? How long has it been?"

We spent the next ten minutes catching up on our lives. Mike shared that he had really struggled back when he attended the church youth group. Reeling from his parents' divorce, he had turned to drugs and alcohol to numb his pain. He even confessed that he was often high when he came to our youth services. His life had continued to deteriorate as he struggled to hold down a job. Two failed marriages and a couple of kids along the way were part of the collateral damage.

"Then one day last year I was moving some boxes in my garage," Mike said, "and found the Bible my mom had given me for my sixteenth birthday. I can't remember ever reading it, let alone taking it to church with me, but I must have, because when I opened it up, there was a note from you that said, 'I know you're hurting. I don't have all the answers, but I know a God who does, and he loves you very much. I'm here if you need to talk,' followed by 'Jeremiah 31:3.' Just out of curiosity, I flipped to that verse. When I read it, I started crying. All of a sudden, I realized that God had always been there, trying to love me, trying to show me the way, protecting me from myself and all the crazy stuff I was into. Well, long story short, I went to church the next Sunday, and that's when I accepted him into my heart as my Lord and Savior."

"Praise God, Mike!" I had tears in my eyes, marveling at God's goodness.

"You probably don't even remember writing that note," Mike went on, "but God used it to speak to me and remind me that he has always loved me. I know I wasn't really involved much in youth group, but I could tell that you really loved all us kids. You wanted us to know how much Jesus loves us. Well, now I know."

CALLED AND COMMANDED

I have to confess that I didn't remember writing that note to Mike. During my youth ministry when I didn't feel as if I was getting through to some of the kids, I would sometimes slip a note of encouragement into their Bibles or backpacks. So even though I didn't think I had made any impact on Mike's life, I later discovered that God used a note that probably took me thirty seconds to write as a reminder of his love for Mike.

Regardless of how we express it, we're called to love others the same way Christ loves us. It's curious, too, when I think about it, because often the words, actions, and moments that mean the most to other people aren't necessarily the same ones I would pick. But we all have the power to influence one another's lives. And that's the beauty of human relationships within the kingdom of God: we're responsible to love others as we love ourselves.

We can't control how, when, or whether they will respond—and fortunately we don't have to. We're just called and commanded by Jesus to love those around us: "A new command I give you: Love one another. As I have loved you, so you must love one another. By this everyone will know that you are my disciples, if you love one another" (John 13:34–35).

Even though we all need other people in our lives, finding a way to love them with the love of Jesus and to trust God for their well-being can still be a challenge. In his Word, God makes it clear that his desire is that all of us will be in a loving relationship with him: "The Lord is not slow in keeping his promise, as some understand slowness. Instead he is patient with you, not wanting anyone to perish, but everyone to come to repentance" (2 Peter 3:9). He pursues us just as a shepherd goes after even one missing sheep, relentless in his quest until he brings each lost lamb home.

Sometimes, however, I suspect we allow our relationships with others to get in the way of our faith in God and where he wants to take us. It may be a matter of caring too much about what others think of us or focusing on ourselves when we should be thinking of others. Like Paul on his voyage to Rome, we must allow God to work in the lives of those around us at his own pace and in his own time. We can't save them, but God can!

CATALYST FOR COURAGE

Trapped in a doozy of a storm, Paul and his shipmates had thrown the cargo and tackle overboard and gone for many days without food when Paul began to share what God had revealed to him. In addition to showing him that everyone onboard would survive, even as the ship wrecked, God had reminded Paul that he was not alone. Not only did he have the loving presence of God with him, but he also had a community of others suffering through the very same storm. Paul's message to his fellow passengers was not only prophetic but also a catalyst for courage:

> Last night an angel of the God to whom I belong and whom I serve stood beside me and said, "Do not be afraid, Paul. You must stand trial before Caesar; and God has graciously given you the lives of all who sail with you." So keep up your courage, men, for I have faith in God that it will happen just as he told me. Nevertheless, we must run aground on some island. (Acts 27:23–26)

When we're consumed and crippled by the storms of life, we sometimes become blinded to the needs of those around us. Even bearing the worst of our own pain, we're never the only ones suffering or in need. Even when we're hurting, we still have a choice to either encourage those around us with our faith or discourage them with our doubt.

Just as faith is contagious, so is fear. If we allow fear and doubt to swallow us, we have nothing to give to those around us. But when we choose to keep going by faith, God can use us to reflect his love, hope, and power to others desperate to experience him. We can be either clogs or conduits.

Paul was a conduit and catalyst to other passengers, reminding them that God had given him courage not only for his own predicament—standing trial before Caesar in Rome—but also for the survival of the others onboard. God told Paul that they would all make it, and that was good enough for Paul!

And it's also good enough for you and me as we interact with others on our own life journeys to our divine destinations. Not only will we survive and thrive, but so will the people accompanying us along the way. God told Paul, "I have given you the lives of all who sail with you. Everyone will make it. They're all going to be okay—I promise."

This message is an important reminder that we all have the ability to positively influence others by our faith and our relationship with God. Our horizontal relationships have vertical consequences, and our vertical relationship has horizontal consequences. The way we love, serve, and pray for those around us has an eternal impact.

ATTITUDE OF ACTION

Paul's message also has significant implications for which relationships we choose to invest in. We must be attentive to those we allow on our ship. Because whether we like it or not, God has given us the lives of those who sail with us. While we can't make decisions for them, we can exert a godly influence and set a Christlike example for them to follow.

Most of us cross paths with a wide variety of people on any given day: other customers in line, people in the same restaurant, coworkers from another department. While these interactions may seem insignificant, you never know when something you say or do will encourage others and point them to God.

So much is made these days of the social, political, racial, and economic divisions in our country, but I know that the love of God and kindness of Christ are also alive and well. It's unfortunate that a small number of people identifying themselves as Christians have created a negative reputation for all of us. If we're serious about our faith and living it out, however, we need to take back the name of Christ follower and show—not just tell—others what the gospel is really about.

This attitude of action applies to all layers of our relational fabric. It includes acquaintances, those people we see regularly in certain situations or contexts, such as work, school, and our neighborhoods. We have opportunities with these people to connect and talk about more than just the common interests that bring us together. Acquaintances can often become friends and confidants—people we trust with more of our lives and, therefore, more of our faith.

Just as Jesus had twelve disciples with whom he experienced consistent, ongoing community, we also need a small number of individuals with whom we can be vulnerable and transparent. Whether it's a group of close friends, a small group from church, or a close-knit neighborhood, we rely on these people for a deeper level of support and encouragement.

Finally, there's family—those people, whether by blood or by bond, with whom we experience lifelong relationships through all the ups and downs of life. These relationships are often the most important as well as the most challenging. We've all experienced both the wounds and the blessings of our families of origin. Sometimes the offenses and scars linger and prevent us from loving family members the way we want to or know we should.

As we mature and develop, we have choices about whether to forgive and ask for forgiveness in order to heal fractured family relationships. Throughout Scripture God repeatedly instructs us to love and forgive one another, indicating that our willingness and ability to do so reflects our capacity to receive the grace and forgiveness he extends to us. We're told, "Whoever claims to love God yet hates a brother or sister is a liar. For whoever does not love their brother and sister, whom they have seen, cannot love God, whom they have not seen" (1 John 4:20).

ENGAGED AND INVESTED

Paul didn't have to share the message God had given to him with his shipmates, but he knew that he could encourage them by doing so. Paul never stopped giving, even during that life-threatening storm. Similarly, doing your part to love the people onboard your ship requires attention and diligence. The bottom line is that all relationships require maintenance. We must not take our loved ones for granted and assume all is well as long as no one's crying, dying, or in jail! Investing in others is not easy, and I caution you to take your commitments, whether to friends or family, very seriously. You have a limited amount of time, energy, and attention to invest, so spend it wisely.

Ignoring the requirements of your relationships can be costly, both for you and the other people. Sometimes we treat our relationships like our cars and have them serviced only when a light pops up on the dashboard or when we break down on the side of the road. Most auto manufacturers exhort owners and drivers to service their vehicles regularly in order to avoid the problems that inevitably come when we wait until we're forced to stop.

I encourage you to be proactive and invest in the lives of the people you care about. They may be hurting and give no outward indications. If they know you accept and love them, however, they may be willing to share their burdens before they snowball into avalanches. You must be engaged and invested in order for your relationships to grow and deepen.

If you have a spouse, he or she will require your attention and service. Kids definitely require your full engagement. Even pets require maintenance! If you have a dog, cat, or simply a goldfish, you have to provide ongoing attention and care or it will die. The more relationships you have, the more time and resources you must budget to meet relational responsibilities. Avoid taking on more than your ship can hold. Always count the cost of your relational investment and the necessary maintenance *before* you commit to new people.

Despite how nomadic our culture has become, there's a connection we enjoy with family, in part due to online connectivity, that keeps us grounded and provides a shelter and foundation for who we are and what we're about. In the past, and even still in many cultures throughout the world, multiple generations all lived under one roof, sharing, suffering, and celebrating whatever they encountered. While this may not be feasible in your life for a number of reasons, I encourage you not to overlook parents, grandparents, and other extended family members.

And don't rely on technology alone to convey your love and maintain your relationships. An emoji is no substitute for a hug or your heart.

CONNECTED OR ENTANGLED

In our technologically advanced, social media–saturated society, we're seemingly more connected than ever. We can chat with friends in Singapore via video calling, text with loved ones in our hometown, and follow the people we admire most on Twitter. But I'm not convinced all this connectivity is actually making our relationships stronger. Sometimes we lose our connections to one another as we become more entangled in technology. In all our online connecting, are we missing out on what matters most—true friendship, authentic fellowship, and healthy intimacy?

We've all seen commercials for tech companies such as Apple, Samsung, and Verizon showcasing the way their products and services keep us connected with a simple call, text, Skype, chat, post, or click. Although our ability to stay in touch with others is enhanced by technology, it's not the same thing as actually sitting across from someone over a meal and sharing from the heart.

It's great to view a child's birthday party via video, but it's not the same as being there to taste the cake, hold the little one, feel her breath blowing out the candles, and hear her joy as she unwraps presents. I know it's incredibly cost efficient to conduct videoconferences with important clients and team members, but often you still need those face-to-face encounters to convey more than what can be read from a report or analyzed in a spreadsheet. As much as our tech providers and online-service companies want us to believe we're personally connected across the miles, it's not the same as being there.

While our longing to connect with others remains as strong as ever, the constant fragmentation of our schedules can make it tough to maintain strong personal ties. We've all experienced those moments in a group, or even our own families, when all the people in the room are looking down, glued to their phones or tablets.

Please understand that I'm not anti-technology; in fact, I'm one of its biggest fans and most frequent users. My phone and laptop allow me to communicate while traveling and ministering around the world. However, I always try to remember that constant access does not necessarily create stronger bonds. We have to make sure we stay in control of our tech devices if we want to enjoy the quality of relationships that enrich our lives and allow us to enhance the lives of others.

Today there is tremendous pressure to work hard at all hours and be connected 24/7. In so many ways, technology remains an amazing blessing for human beings, but like anything, it must be kept in check, submitted to God's authority and guidance, and used appropriately. Our phones can easily become idols if we let them. And this hurts not only us and our relationship with God but also all our other relationships. There's no substitute for sitting across from a Christian brother as he asks your advice on an issue he's facing with his kids, sharing a meal with team members to celebrate a milestone achieved, or shaking the hand of a new neighbor.

> **True friendship is about more than texting and sharing photos online.**

Words such as *friend* and *follower* have gained new meanings in our online world, but we should never forget their primary definitions. True friendship is about more than texting and sharing photos online. And following others must never take the place of following Jesus first.

God has entrusted you with certain people in your life, and he loves them just as much as he loves you. He's also given you the unique privilege of loving and serving these individuals. Whether it's for a limited season or for a lifetime, you have people on your boat traveling with you right now. Your divine destination may not be the same as theirs, but your fates are intertwined.

Now is the time to encourage them and remind them that you're blessed to have them riding spiritual shotgun with you. Now is the time to tell them—and, more importantly, show them—just how much you love them.

They have their Rome, and you have yours. And even if a ship sinks, everyone is going to get there!

SHAKE FREE . . . FROM WORRYING ABOUT OTHERS

The following questions are intended to help you reflect on your relationships, let go of your worries about them, and trust God with the people in your life.

1. What relationships do you worry about most right now? Why? What is the source of your concern?

2. Who are the people who have sustained your journey in the past? How did they support you—emotionally, materially, spiritually? Other ways? What difference did their support make in your life? How has their encouragement affected your relationship with God?

3. Whom in your life do you need to encourage today? How can you reflect God's love in these people's lives to help them keep going? Call or text right now to let them know you're thinking about them. Then follow through with an invitation for lunch, coffee, or some time together in fellowship.

God, you know I'm prone to worry, especially about the people in my life, so today I cast my cares on you and surrender my loved ones to you, trusting that you will guide, protect, and love them the same way you do for me. For the ones who do not know you, allow them to see your goodness and mercy reflected in our relationship. And for my other sisters and brothers in Christ, may I be an encourager and supporter in the faith. Thank you for these wonderful and special people near to me, Lord. I'm so blessed to have them. Amen.

7

God Has
No Plan B

It is wonderful what miracles God works in
wills that are utterly surrendered to Him.

—Hannah Whitall Smith,
The Christian's Secret of a Happy Life

My old tennis racket from high school. A wobbly sled that hadn't seen a snowy hillside in years. Boxes of textbooks. A set of china from my wife's great aunt. Three kids' backpacks in various states of deterioration. One spare tire and three bicycles.

It's amazing what you can accumulate in your garage and attic—let alone the rest of the house—over the years, but there's something about moving from one home to another that forces you to let go of things. And it's rarely easy, at least from my experience.

When my young family moved from Pennsylvania to California many years ago, it felt as if we were preparing for an expedition to Mount Everest. There were the items we chose to take because they were useful, such as beds, mattresses, chairs, our sofa, and the kitchen table. Then we packed things our kids wanted to hold on to, such as favorite toys, stuffed animals, and home-made artwork. Practical necessities from the kitchen—dishes, pots, and pans—certainly came with us.

Our list of items to move grew until one day I sat down with Eva and said,

"This is crazy! We can't take all this stuff with us. We've got to focus on essentials. This is our chance to start over and get more organized."

She agreed, but it was easier said than done. What if we needed that snowblower in Sacramento? Couldn't it snow there sometimes? Or what if one of the kids wanted to take boxing lessons down the road? Shouldn't we keep that punching bag and gloves somebody gave us?

Plus, we wanted to make the transition as smooth as possible for our kids. If hanging on to a life-sized stuffed pink panda made my daughter happy, then so be it. What's one more stuffed pink panda bear, right? Those panda bears add up, though—especially with three kids—and soon we were drowning in stuff once again.

We had to learn what it meant to "cut our lifeboats" and let them drift away.

TRAVELING LIGHT

It's not necessarily bad to have a lot of stuff, but it can quickly accumulate and get in the way of our willingness to go where God wants us to go, when he wants us to go, and how he wants us to get there. Traveling light seems to be the best way to proceed on our journeys to Rome, but sometimes we forget the weight of all the possessions, responsibilities, and expectations we're carrying. We become so encumbered by what we've accumulated, both materially and emotionally, that it's more challenging than necessary to follow God. We may even know we're getting in our own way as we venture to Rome, but we've become accustomed to all the stuff we're carrying.

This attitude is often reinforced by our culture. After the Great Depression that many of our parents and grandparents experienced and after the uncertainty of World War II, we slowly slipped into the age of advertising and the mind-set that more is always better. More money, more possessions, more trophies of convenience and status. We see this material frame of mind reflected in the size of our homes and the growth of the billion-dollar storage industry. We have so much stuff that we need to build bigger houses and rent storage units to hold it all.

Lately, however, we're seeing backlash against this more-is-better way of thinking. Apparently, most of us have so much stuff that minimalism—paring possessions down to the basics—has become a popular movement. Best-selling books such as *Minimalism: Live a Meaningful Life* by Joshua Millburn and Ryan Nicodemus, *The Life-Changing Magic of Tidying Up* by Marie Kondo, and *The More of Less* by Joshua Becker address this cultural zeitgeist, this sense that having a lot of stuff—which our culture has encouraged us to do for so long—ultimately won't fulfill us.

I call this longing in so many people the never-enough syndrome. No matter how much money they have, how many achievements, and how many exclusive experiences, they still don't feel satisfied or content with their lives. No matter what they attain—or get rid of—it's never enough. And it's nothing new. Human beings have always struggled with depending on money and material things rather than the living God and his plans for their lives.

> **Our joyful, peace-filled satisfaction comes from knowing and following Jesus.**

As followers of Jesus, you and I know that material possessions can never address the spiritual hunger and thirst each person has to know God and be in relationship with him. When Jesus said, "I have come that they may have life, and have it to the full" (John 10:10), he was referring to the passion, purpose, and power we experience when his Spirit dwells in us and we depend on God. Our joyful, peace-filled satisfaction comes from knowing and following Jesus, fulfilling the purpose for which our Creator designed us. But we're also not immune to the human tendency to measure God's favor by the material blessings in our lives.

While God often blesses us with tangible evidence of his love and favor, this doesn't necessarily mean earthly riches. It's not that money and wealth are wrong or evil in and of themselves; the problem lies in our human propensity to make them what we worship. Jesus said, "No one can serve two masters. Either you will hate the one and love the other, or you will be devoted to the one and despise the other. You cannot serve both God and money" (Matthew 6:24).

When you become accustomed to having a lot of money, it's tempting to become dependent on the sense of security, comfort, convenience, power, and entitlement that typically comes with it. We start feeling in control of our lives and able to use money to solve problems and buy happiness. No wonder Jesus also said, "It is easier for a camel to go through the eye of a needle than for someone who is rich to enter the kingdom of God" (19:24).

Again, it's not that being rich is sinful; it's simply that wealth fosters a sense of independence, autonomy, and confidence in our own abilities rather than in God's. Letting go of such self-sufficiency can be painful.

Just ask the wealthy man, sometimes called the rich young ruler, who visited Christ in hopes of becoming his disciple:

> A man came up to Jesus and asked, "Teacher, what good thing must
> I do to get eternal life?"
>
> "Why do you ask me about what is good?" Jesus replied.
> "There is only One who is good. If you want to enter life, keep
> the commandments."

"Which ones?" he inquired.

Jesus replied, "'You shall not murder, you shall not commit adultery, you shall not steal, you shall not give false testimony, honor your father and mother,' and 'love your neighbor as yourself.'"

"All these I have kept," the young man said. "What do I still lack?"

Jesus answered, "If you want to be perfect, go, sell your possessions and give to the poor, and you will have treasure in heaven. Then come, follow me."

When the young man heard this, he went away sad, because he had great wealth. (19:16–22)

Please understand what Jesus meant here by the original Greek word translated "perfect." *Teleios* is defined as "lacking nothing necessary to completeness."* It doesn't so much mean "perfect" as you or I might think of it but rather that sense of development, wholeness, and contentment that comes from knowing and following God, which is what we see in the context of this passage. It had already been established in Jesus's conversation with this young man that he kept the Ten Commandments, so the only thing left in developing his spiritual maturity was to shift the focus of his wealth from earth to heaven.

It wasn't the fact that he was rich that was causing him to be sad. It was his *love* of money, as well as Jesus's awareness of his dependence on wealth as his lifeboat for life's storms. Paul himself wrote, "For the love of money is a root of all kinds of evil. Some people, eager for money, have wandered from the faith and pierced themselves with many griefs" (1 Timothy 6:10).

Christ asked the man to let go of everything else in order to take up his cross and follow Jesus as his Lord. In other words, he asked him to give away his possessions and no longer allow them to have any hold on his life.

---

* Blue Letter Bible, s.v. *"teleios,"* www.blueletterbible.org/lang/lexicon/lexicon.cfm?Strongs=G5046&t=KJV.

To relinquish his reliance on money.

To give up always having a plan B.

PLAN G

Do you usually have a plan B in mind as you look at your day and what you think you'll be facing? Or do you usually wing it and improvise as you go along? Or are you able to commit each day to God and just allow it to unfold without relying on a plan B? While our personalities play a part in whether we tend to be careful planners or spontaneous doers, we're usually encouraged to plan ahead and look before we leap.

Most of us have been taught to build our lives around planning, preparation, and precaution as keys to stable, successful lives. We've learned to create contingency plans so that when life doesn't go as expected—when we find ourselves caught in storms—we have options and resources to see us through. If we lose our jobs, we have enough money saved up to help us until we find a new one. If unexpected guests drop by, we have enough food on hand to include them for dinner. If our flight to the business meeting gets canceled, we just participate via videoconference.

It's a plan B mentality that's quite pervasive. In fact, as responsible adults, we're told by numerous sources, from parents to self-help gurus, that we should save money for retirement, keep our kitchen pantries stocked at all times, and buy bigger clothes for the kids at the end of each season for next year. We should keep cash on hand for emergencies, pay bills ahead of time when possible, and buy new tires for our cars before we actually need them. We should make our wills and store them safely along with instructions for the funerals we've already paid for, buy Christmas presents months in advance, and set goals for our careers and create strategies to attain them.

I'm not sure how many people actually operate this way, but you can't deny that we live in a culture that encourages us to be prepared and in control. Or maybe it's just human nature to anticipate the future and plan according to what we expect to happen based on past experiences. While we know we can't control what the future holds, I suspect being able to predict what we'll face each day comforts us.

If we know what to expect, we can plan accordingly and feel in control of our lives. We don't have to face the possibility of painful, unexpected events or encounters. We don't have to worry about shipwrecks and storms because we have a lifeboat. In short, if we think we know what tomorrow holds, we don't have to live by faith. We can keep coming up with a plan B instead of living by plan G—God's perfect plan for our lives.

Let It Go

Letting go of plan B and stepping out in faith to follow plan G require courage. It's one thing to follow God when life is good and your circumstances are stable, if not predictable. But it takes a deep-rooted faith in the goodness, power, and sovereignty of God to ditch plan B when you're caught in the storm and feel as though your ship is crashing and you're about to go overboard. That was the situation Paul and his shipmates faced while trapped by this hurricane that lasted more than *two weeks*. The narrative continues,

> On the fourteenth night we were still being driven across the Adriatic
> Sea, when about midnight the sailors sensed they were approaching
> land. They took soundings and found that the water was a hundred
> and twenty feet deep. A short time later they took soundings again
> and found it was ninety feet deep. Fearing that we would be dashed
> against the rocks, they dropped four anchors from the stern and prayed
> for daylight. In an attempt to escape from the ship, the sailors let the

lifeboat down into the sea, pretending they were going to lower some anchors from the bow. Then Paul said to the centurion and the soldiers, "Unless these men stay with the ship, you cannot be saved." So the soldiers cut the ropes that held the lifeboat and let it drift away. (Acts 27:27–32)

Notice here that some sailors attempted to deceive the centurion by saying they were going to lower anchors, when actually they were preparing the lifeboat for their escape. We've already established the level of desperation experienced by the crew onboard this ship—and who wouldn't feel hopeless after two weeks in the middle of this terrible northeaster? So when the soldiers responded to Paul's warning by cutting the ropes, releasing the lifeboat, and letting it drift away, I'm guessing many of those aboard the ship felt as though they were also losing their last shot at survival. If ever it was time to use a lifeboat, it was then!

But instead, this crazy God-following, Jesus-preaching prisoner kept telling them to do the opposite of the logical procedure in such a storm. Paul knew we often have to abandon our own plans, no matter how logical or well thought out, in order to follow God's plan. Paul knew what we, too, often discover today on our individual journeys to the "Rome" God has for us: the power to let go and move forward is as important as the power to hold on and be still.

As long as you continue to rely on your own plans, as long as you go out of your way to ensure that you get what you think you want no matter what it takes, you will never experience the abundant adventure of faith God has for you. Jesus tells us, "Whoever wants to save their life will lose it, but whoever loses their life for me will find it" (Matthew 16:25).

You must let go of what you think you want in order to get what your heart craves most. You must relinquish self-reliance in order to enjoy intimate reliance on the One who loves you most. You can go down with your own ship or grab God's hand. But you can't do both. You can't serve two masters.

You will never reach your destination until you let go of your lifeboat.

You will never reach your destination until you let go of plan B.

God doesn't want to touch your circumstance; he wants to transform your life.

It may be good to have a plan B in business. It's great to be prepared if you're in the Boy Scouts. But on your Christian walk, it's God or nothing! He is your plan A, plan B, plan C—there can be no other plan. If you want to get to Rome, you must let go of the security blanket of alternate plans and trust God as your one and only plan.

> ## You can go down with your own ship or grab God's hand.

So what stops us? Too often I fear we spend more time attempting to *understand* God than choosing to *trust* him. Somehow we believe that if we can comprehend what God is up to, then we can obey him and go where he wants us to go. We think that if we know his motives and how his plans all come together, then we can comply. But God's ways are not our ways, and his thoughts are not our thoughts (see Isaiah 55:8).

Faith does not require you to understand God. Faith requires you to trust him. His Word makes this clear: "Trust in the LORD with all your heart and lean not on your own understanding" (Proverbs 3:5). Our blessing takes place when we shift from listening to God's Word to obeying it.

Understanding God is not a prerequisite for trusting him. You don't have to understand the engineering principles at work in order to fly in a plane; you simply have to trust the construction, mechanics, and pilot jetting you across the sky. You don't need to comprehend astrophysics to delight in the awe-inspiring beauty of a black night sky salted with stars.

I know it's not easy to trust. So many people have let you down. So many events have caught you off guard. So many betrayals have blindsided you. Somewhere inside, you built a lifeboat and vowed never to allow others to rock it. But that defensive posture—perhaps even one that was necessary to survive in the past—no longer serves you. It's time to let go of all the lifeboats and plan Bs you've accumulated to safeguard your heart. In the words of that classic song from the Disney movie, "Let it go!"

Let go of that relationship that's holding you back.

Let go of that memory.

Let go of that experience.

Let go of that trauma.

Let go of that idol, whether money or something else.

Let go of *anything* you're relying on instead of God.

Let it all drift away!

SHAKE FREE . . . FROM CONTROL

Take some time alone with God to answer the following questions and reflect on your answers. Listen for God's voice as you examine what you need to relinquish in order to reach your Rome.

1. Do you typically have some kind of plan B for the events and people you expect to encounter each day? How well has having a plan B worked for you so far? When and how has it been helpful? When has it prevented you from trusting God fully?

2. How much do you rely on money as your plan B to help you get through life? How has viewing money this way influenced your decisions and the directions you've taken? Is there a problem or area in your life right now for which you're viewing money as the solution instead of seeking God's direction?

3. What lifeboat do you need to cut and let drift away in your life? How do you typically rely on it instead of God? What are you afraid will happen if you let it go?

Dear Lord, I come before you right now, knowing you're aware of all the ways I cling to my own lifeboats instead of trusting you to see me through life's storms. Too often, God, I allow my fears to motivate my decisions and actions, worrying about the future and anticipating the worst that could happen instead of trusting you for your best. Instead, I want to trust you completely—to reach the Rome you have for me. Empower me with your Holy Spirit to overcome my fear, my self-reliance, and my dependence on anything and anyone other than you. Even if my ship wrecks, Lord, I would rather be with you on rough seas than on a pleasure cruise without you. Help me trust you even though I may never understand you. Thank you for saving me and seeing me through all the storms—the ones in the past, the ones around me now, and the ones to come. Amen.

8

God Does Great Things with Broken Pieces

Leave the broken, irreversible past in God's hands, and step out into the invincible future with Him.

—Oswald Chambers, *My Utmost for His Highest*

So many of my personal heroes of the faith overcame impossible odds to fulfill the purpose God had for them. Like Paul, they endured storms, shipwrecks, and snakebites that left them wondering how God was going to do the impossible and get them to Rome. Through ordeals and obstacles, tempests and trials, they never stopped trusting God to keep his promises.

Such faith is easy to talk about but hard to exercise when your ship is falling apart because of a storm. As I write this, civil unrest and racial division simmer in our country, fueled by riots, shootings, and politics. Just as historic strides were slowly being made toward unity, incendiary issues and incidents now spark the emotional tinderbox of so many people and threaten to spread like wildfire, blocking our country's path toward unified advancement. Despite unexpected prejudice and unthinkable injustice, however, God is still at work and intent on bringing about miraculous change, equality, and harmony.

If you struggle to believe me, just consider the story of a man imprisoned for no other reason than the color of his skin. While I have suffered my share of prejudice, I have never endured what this man faced. As I mentioned earlier, growing up as a minority in Pennsylvania's Lehigh Valley wasn't easy, but the taunts, insults, and slights I received don't compare to being imprisoned—for *twenty-seven years.*

POWER FROM THE PIECES

Twenty-seven years of staring at cement walls and iron bars. Twenty-seven years without the privileges and preferences you and I take for granted. Twenty-seven years of keeping the spark of a dream alive. I can't imagine how a person could not abandon hope as days, weeks, and months accrete into years and then decades of racially motivated incarceration.

And how would one cope with the unfairness, the injustice of it all? As much as I want to follow Jesus and trust God, I wonder whether I would have the fortitude to resist anger, hatred, and bitterness for all those years. I wonder whether, locked away and forgotten in a cell, I would be able to trust God to get me to Rome. I wonder whether I could resist the temptation to seethe with a desire for violence and vengeance.

But Nelson Mandela did. Instead of brooding, moping, and resigning himself to defeat, he focused on completing a law degree to complement his prior experience as an activist and reformer. He remained in contact with other conduits for change even amid the atrocities of apartheid. He refused to believe that the government of his beloved South Africa could not become a beacon of democracy for the world. He channeled his energies toward being the catalyst for change he had proclaimed in his famous "Speech from the Dock" at his trial in 1964:

> I have fought against white domination, and I have fought against black
> domination. I have cherished the ideal of a democratic and free society
> in which all persons live together in harmony and with equal opportuni-

ties. It is an ideal which I hope to live for and to achieve. But if needs be, it is an ideal for which I am prepared to die.*

Even when faced with prostate cancer and tuberculosis, Mandela never gave up the faith that one day he would not only be released from prison but also be able to lead the people of his nation—all people of all colors—to unity like that democratic, free ideal he had dreamed about his entire life.

When he was finally released in 1990, Mandela was over seventy years old, but his age and health challenges did not impede his determination to lead his country to a new day of justice and equality for all. Three years after leaving prison, Mandela was awarded the Nobel Peace Prize for his efforts. And the following year, in 1994, he was elected South Africa's president in his nation's historic first multiracial election.

Throughout his lifetime, Nelson Mandela continued to make choices about what to do with the broken pieces of his life. He could use them as reasons to give up hope, or he could use them as tools for transformation. He could suffer his shattering in silence, or he could continue to voice prayers of praise. He could mourn those broken pieces and fixate on his pain, or he could turn them over to God and allow him to create something miraculous.

You have the same power to choose what to do with your own broken pieces.

You can despair over the wreckage, or you can allow God to create something new.

LAST SUPPER

Perhaps nowhere in Scripture is this choice we all face illustrated as well as in Paul's shipwreck on the way to Rome. I imagine that once the lifeboat had been

---

* Nelson Mandela, "Biography of Nelson Mandela," Nelson Mandela Foundation, www.nelsonmandela.org /content/page/biography.

cut loose and allowed to drift away, many of the passengers assumed they were about to die. Their only chance at survival had been thrown away, and the storm to end all storms had raged for two weeks. Everyone onboard was exhausted physically and emotionally, which might explain why Paul encouraged his fellow passengers to eat something despite the situation:

> Just before dawn Paul urged them all to eat. "For the last fourteen days," he said, "you have been in constant suspense and have gone without food—you haven't eaten anything. Now I urge you to take some food. You need it to survive. Not one of you will lose a single hair from his head." After he said this, he took some bread and gave thanks to God in front of them all. Then he broke it and began to eat. They were all encouraged and ate some food themselves. Altogether there were 276 of us on board. When they had eaten as much as they wanted, they lightened the ship by throwing the grain into the sea. (Acts 27:33–38)

If these 275 other people thought Paul was a little loony when he warned them to stay with the ship, his next instruction would have confirmed it. After all they had been through for the past two weeks, despite their assumption that they were about to die, Paul wanted them to stop and have a bite to eat! Surely his request must have seemed like asking someone to rearrange deck chairs on the *Titanic,* as the old saying goes. Why in the world should they force themselves to eat just as the ship was about to wreck? After all, they apparently had not been hungry enough to eat during the storm's duration.

But there was a method to Paul's apparent madness. His "last supper" invitation was the practical means to further God's supernatural miracle. Paul told them, "I urge you to take some food. You need it to survive. Not one of you will lose a single hair from his head" (verse 34). Notice his logic here, if you'll indulge my paraphrase: "I want you to eat because your body needs fuel. It's essential for your survival—and you *are* going to survive!"

Paul didn't waver in his trust that God would deliver everyone safely to shore. But Paul also knew that practical matters such as nourishment cannot be ignored. Did the people onboard have to eat in order for God to save them? No, of course not. God is all powerful and can do anything he wants.

So why should these passengers eat first? Because we have to do our part in order to receive the blessings God has for us. We have to be willing to receive what the Lord wants to give us. We have to maintain our strength in order to cling to God's hand as he delivers us from our shipwrecks. We need to do what it takes to keep going on a practical level, even as we wait on God to propel us forward.

For Paul's shipmates, eating this meal gave them energy for what was about to happen. Sometimes we have to demonstrate our faith by getting ready for what we know God wants to do in our lives. He can't heal our marriages if we're not willing to talk to our spouses. He can't turn around our finances if we're not willing to address our shopping addictions. He can't shape the broken pieces of our lives into our rescue rafts if we're not willing to yield to his direction.

God will not transform your life if you won't let him.

You have to do your part if you want to reach Rome, because God always does his part!

BROKENNESS BEFORE THE BREAKTHROUGH

Even once you choose to allow God to build something new from your broken pieces, you have to keep trusting him each step of the way. Paul convinced the others onboard to eat and regain their strength—right before tossing the rest of their grain overboard to lighten the ship (see Acts 27:38). The storm then began to dissipate. Another long night had passed, and at long last they saw the shore:

> When daylight came, they did not recognize the land, but they saw a bay with a sandy beach, where they decided to run the ship aground if they could. Cutting loose the anchors, they left them in the sea and at the same time untied the ropes that held the rudders. Then they hoisted the foresail to the wind and made for the beach. But the ship struck a sandbar and ran aground. The bow stuck fast and would not move, and the stern was broken to pieces by the pounding of the surf.
>
> The soldiers planned to kill the prisoners to prevent any of them from swimming away and escaping. But the centurion wanted to spare Paul's life and kept them from carrying out their plan. He ordered those who could swim to jump overboard first and get to land. The rest were to get there on planks or on other pieces of the ship. In this way everyone reached land safely. (verses 39–44)

Finally, they spotted land! They cut the anchors, untied the rudders, and hoisted the sail in an attempt to reach shore. But Paul and his fellow prisoners weren't out of danger yet. The soldiers onboard decided to kill them rather than risk letting them escape! I told you that this story was better than any Jason Bourne movie!

These soldiers were probably just doing their jobs; I doubt they had a desire to kill the prisoners or they would have already tossed them overboard in the storm. With shore in sight, though, it was a different situation. If the prisoners under their charge escaped, the soldiers knew they would likely be killed themselves. But God saved Paul and the others through the protective mercy of the centurion, Julius, who had been placed in charge back at the beginning of their voyage (see verse 1).

So often, just as your ship is about to go down, you spot the shore—only to encounter a new barrier. After months of unemployment, the job that seemed perfect for you on Friday goes to someone else on Monday. After recovering from a debilitating injury, you discover a suspicious spot that requires a biopsy. After years of rebuilding your credit score, you fall prey to identity theft as a cybercriminal wreaks havoc on your accounts.

It's one of the Enemy's oldest tricks in the book: just as we finally take a long-awaited step forward, we suddenly face being pushed two steps back. The devil believes if he can pull the rug out from under us one more time, perhaps we will give up hope in God and abandon our faith.

When God wants you to go to Rome, though, no ploy of Satan can prevent it! What happened as the ship ran aground on a sandbar and got pummeled into pieces by the surf? They were close enough to shore that they could use pieces of the ship's wreckage to help them swim and float to get there. Their brokenness became their breakthrough!

> **God can do great things with your broken pieces!**

The same is true for you. God will use pieces of your wreckage to get you to shore. No matter what mistakes you've made or what detours you've taken while straying from where God wants you to be, it's not too late. No matter what you've said or haven't said, what you've done or haven't done. No matter the depth of your pain, fear, or anxiety. No matter how dark your secret or how terrible your addiction. God can do great things with your broken pieces!

If you will yield your shipwreck to God, he can create an ark bigger than Noah's to guide you through the floodwaters rising around you. The Lord has not brought you this far to let you flounder and sink a few feet from shore. God has sustained you and protected you and carried you through the storms to get you to where you are right now. He has a purpose for you, and you will get to Rome if you surrender the wreckage in your life to him.

MIRACLES ARE THE MOSAICS

God's purposes are greater than our brokenness. We're assured in his Word that he is with us and will never give up on us: "We are pressed on every side by troubles, but we are not crushed. We are perplexed, but not driven to despair. We are hunted down, but never abandoned by God. We get knocked down, but we are not destroyed" (2 Corinthians 4:8–9, NLT).

Notice what this passage says we may face: troubles on every side, feeling perplexed, being hunted, and even getting knocked down. But we will not be crushed, driven to despair, abandoned, or destroyed. What a powerful promise from the living God to his people! "No word from God will ever fail" (Luke 1:37).

If it's broken, God can fix it.

If it's empty, God can fill it.

If it failed, God can restore it.

If it's sin, God can forgive it.

If it's wrong, God can make it right.

If it's crooked, God can make it straight.

If it fell, God can pick it up.

If it's paralyzed, God can make it move.

Even if it's dead, God can resurrect it!

Nothing is beyond God.

Nothing is impossible with God!

Have you ever seen a mosaic, perhaps in a museum or in the patio or walls of someone's garden? Mosaic is an ancient art form that uses small stones, tiles, or broken shards to create a much larger design or portrait. I love looking at a mosaic and thinking about how something so beautiful comes from all those hundreds if not thousands of little pieces that, by themselves, would be unexceptional or even ugly. That's the way God creates his masterpiece from our messiness. Miracles are the mosaics God forms from the broken pieces of our lives.

Maybe you're struggling to see the beautiful mosaic pattern God is creating from your broken pieces. Will you trust him even if parts of your life look dirty and broken, shattered and scarred? Remember, you don't have to be perfect to call upon the name of Jesus. You simply have to acknowledge your brokenness. You have only to admit that you can't keep your ship together any longer in the midst of the storm. I have seen drunks and drug addicts call upon the name of Jesus and watched as their lives and circumstances changed. I have met former dealers and dopers, prostitutes and pimps whose lives have been radically transformed by the power of God.

You don't have to be perfect when you call upon the name of Jesus, because that name is perfect all by itself. You just have to cry out to him and acknowledge your need. When broken people call upon God, his blessings break through.

If you're struggling to stay afloat, grab a plank and trust God to get you to shore. On Paul's ship, almost three hundred men survived because they could swim or cling to remnants of their wrecked ship. They made it to shore only because they held on to little pieces of wood. Those planks, each probably weighing only a tenth or less of what an adult might weigh, could float and keep them from going under.

In full disclosure, I am here today sharing this with you because I, too, have held on to a piece of wood. I'm able to come alongside you with the hope-filled power of God's promises only because of what I cling to every day: the cross of

Christ. "Jesus said to his disciples, 'If any of you wants to be my follower, you must give up your own way, take up your cross, and follow me'" (Matthew 16:24, NLT).

WORSHIP WITH YOUR WOUNDS

God uses broken pieces to carry you home. It may look like a wreck, but it will save your life. When you trust him with the shards of your shame, you discover the freedom, the buoyancy, to rise above the waves and know that you will make it to shore. You may not be able to see how you will get there, but God has provided all you need. Grasping the power of God's promises, you can be like Paul and refuse to panic while those around you fear for their lives. When you give God your broken pieces, you learn to

- worship with your wounds
- praise with your problems
- move with your mess
- rejoice in the ruckus
- sing through the sorrow
- dance in the drought

Knowing what you know about what God has promised, your circumstances should not change your praise, but your praise can change your circumstances. Your praise reminds you of your Father, the almighty God, Creator of heaven and earth, who loved you enough to sacrifice his Son on two beams of wood. If God loves you this much, will he not provide the lifeline you need right now?

God knows your strengths and your weaknesses, your faith and your fears, your dreams and your nightmares—and he still loves you! His grace and mercy have no limits. His love for you is unconditional. No life is beyond hope, because no life is beyond the reach of our loving, forgiving, and redeeming God.

"'For I know the plans I have for you,' declares the LORD, 'plans to prosper you and not to harm you, plans to give you hope and a future'" (Jeremiah 29:11).

Therefore, no matter how powerless you feel, keep on praising. No matter how messed up your life seems, keep on praying. No matter how broken you are, keep on believing. For at the end of the day, those who sing in the desert will dance in the Promised Land.

Give God the broken pieces, cling to the truth of his promises, and watch what he will do!

SHAKE FREE . . . FROM DESPAIR

Use the following questions to examine some of the broken pieces of your life as you surrender them to God. Trust that no matter how messy past wreckage may be, God is creating his masterful mosaic.

1. As you look back on your life, when have you seen God transform your mistakes into his miracles? How has he redeemed certain painful events to strengthen your heart and grow your faith?

2. What area of brokenness in your life is presently the most difficult for you to give to God? Why? What impact has this struggle to relinquish all areas had on your relationship with him?

3. Spend a few minutes in silence, asking God's Spirit to reveal any broken pieces that need to be surrendered. Write them down in the space that follows. Do any of these surprise you? Why or why not?

Holy Spirit, I thank you for speaking to my heart and revealing the broken pieces that continue to hinder my journey of faith. Please heal those places inside me that continue to ache. I give them all to you right now, even if I can't imagine how you could ever redeem such losses and liabilities. I praise you, Lord, for your love, your power, and your ability to do the impossible. Help me cling to the truth of the promises in your Word rather than obsess about the wreckage floating around me. You always provide a way, Lord, and I know you will continue to give me what I need. I know that you will carry me to shore. Thank you for your cross, which I claim and cling to right now. I know I'm on my way to Rome and nothing can stop me! Amen.

9

In Christ You're Safely Onshore

Through many dangers, toils and snares,
I have already come;
'Tis grace hath brought me safe thus far,
And grace will lead me home.

—John Newton, "Amazing Grace"

T here's something inspiring about visiting Washington, DC. Maybe it's the numerous monuments honoring our country's Founding Fathers and their vision for a nation where all citizens enjoy freedom, equality, and justice. Perhaps it's our capital's design with all those rectangular blocks and (mostly) easy-to-follow numbered streets reflecting an ideal of perfection and symmetry. Of course, it could simply be an awareness of all the amazing moments and world-changing decisions that have taken place there.

All these factors and more came to mind the first time I visited Washington, DC, to meet with a sitting president. At the beginning of this book, I shared my most recent visit, but I was also blessed to participate in the inaugural festivities of the previous administration. Then, I wasn't on the podium where the swearing-in took place. Instead, I participated in the service at St. John's Episcopal Church, a National Historic Landmark, near Lafayette Square across from the White House.

Every US president, from James Madison to the present, has attended St. John's since its construction in 1816. Most presidents from that time on have attended a special service at this grand old church on their Inauguration Day, and that is why I was there: to offer a prayer for the man about to take office. I was both honored and nervous.

It was an experience of firsts for me, as I was the first Hispanic evangelical pastor to be invited to contribute to such a service. It wasn't my first time to visit DC, but it was my first time to officially participate in a presidential inauguration. While I usually don't struggle to keep my ego in check, I have to say that experience caused me to step back and consider how far I had come.

I felt a little like Peter walking on water at the Lord's command. Never in a million years did I expect to be shaking the president's hand along with so many dignitaries, leaders, and celebrities. When I'm not in the pulpit on fire with a message God has ignited in my heart, I'm actually quiet and laid back. So mingling with so many important people at such a momentous event took my breath away.

I remember flying home and feeling so honored and important after that weekend in January. God had chosen me not just to pastor a church or serve as president of a national ministry but also to meet presidents and world changers. Who was I, a computer nerd whose most exciting celebrity moment up until that time had been getting Leonard Nimoy's signature at a sci-fi convention, to be in such illustrious company?

Once I got home, it didn't take me long to find out.

HUMBLED AT HOME

When I landed back in Sacramento, I didn't expect others to treat me any differently—or so I thought. I mean, I was the same husband, father, pastor, and leader I had been before, right? Being in the national spotlight didn't mean I was any more important than anyone else; God had simply blessed me with this unbelievable experience at the inauguration. But the next day I discovered how much my head had swollen.

At breakfast my wife said, "Honey, I know you're busy, and I hate to ask, but my car's making that funny noise again. Would you mind taking it to the mechanic for me?" Then just as I was about to head out the door, my son said, "Dad, are you still planning to come to my game tomorrow?"

As I drove my wife's car to my office, planning to visit the mechanic later in the day, one of the elders at our church called to remind me of a meeting with community leaders from other churches in our area. Stalled in morning rush-hour traffic, I glanced at my phone to find a dozen emails requesting urgent replies, as well as a reminder about my dentist appointment the next day. To top it all off, I realized I still had a sermon to write in addition to all these other activities.

Just as traffic began to move again, I noticed the "check engine" light blinking and heard the engine sputter. And that's when I had to laugh. No matter how important I might have thought I was, the Lord seemed to be reminding me that I was indeed the same man I had been before my trip to Washington.

Later, sitting in the waiting area at the dealership while my wife's car was being repaired, I thought of one of my favorite verses: "Humble yourselves before the Lord, and he will lift you up" (James 4:10). I vowed in that moment that no matter how high—or low—God might take me, I would never let pride sneak into my attitude.

Whether I become a pauper or the president himself, I never want to forget how privileged I am to serve my family, friends, and God's people. No matter how busy I might become, I still want my wife to ask me for help with her car and my son to ask me to go to his ball game. In many ways my trip to Washington, DC, represented the pinnacle of my life as a Christian leader. But in many other ways—which I discovered once I was back home—it reminded me of where I always want to be: following Jesus.

IF ONLY

Being humbled after my meeting with the president reminds me of how we often live conditionally. We chase after the next achievement, the next trophy, the next milestone, the next one-of-a-kind experience. There's nothing wrong with striving for excellence, but we can easily become driven by the value we attach to those pinnacle pursuits, losing sight of serving God and instead seeking human validation. We make our contentment conditional and then wonder why we're disappointed and can't enjoy our lives.

As a result we drift into what I call "if only" thinking, missing what we already have as we continually look ahead to what we hope is waiting for us.

If only I could meet the right person and get married, then I'd be happy.

If only I could finish this degree, then my family would know how smart I am.

If only I could get hired for the right job, then others would know I'm successful.

If only I could get that promotion, then others would know how important I am.

If only I could buy my dream house/car/boat/plane/whatever, then I would know I've made it.

If only . . .

Anytime we stake our contentment, self-worth, and happiness on something yet to be attained, we miss out on what God has for us right now. We overlook the many blessings he's already given us. We aren't engaged in the present with the people we love and the work God has given us to do. We can't focus on all we've already attained, because it never seems to be enough to satisfy that longing inside to be recognized, accepted, and adored.

Instead, we're often gazing at someone else's greener grass on Facebook, envying their latest status purchase or exotic vacation. Maybe I'm wrong, because the problem has been around since Cain killed Abel, but our cultural fascination with social media only seems to reinforce this human tendency toward comparison and "if only" living. Between selfies, tweets, pics, and posts, we can easily end up worrying much more about what others think of us and our online persona than what God thinks of us and what he wants us focused on.

God knows what we truly need, and he provides for his children. It's not that he gives us everything we ask for like some spiritual genie or cosmic vending machine. It's that he wants our hearts so aligned with his that we want what he wants: his perfect and glorious will for our lives. Jesus instructed his followers to pray, "Our Father in heaven, hallowed be your name, your kingdom come, your will be done, on earth as it is in heaven" (Matthew 6:9–10). I believe it's no coincidence that *after* we pray for God's will to be done here on earth, we're told to ask, "Give us today our daily bread" (verse 11).

If we're earnestly desiring God's will, we can be content with what he provides for us *today*—not tomorrow, next week, or a year from now or when we get the promotion, meet the right person, buy that dream car, or move to a bigger house.

SAFELY ONSHORE

If anyone knew about being content with what he had in the present moment, it was our shipwreck survivor Paul. After enduring that perilous storm lasting more than two weeks, after running aground and watching the ship splinter like a twig, after swimming to shore or clinging to planks from the wreckage, Paul and the other passengers *finally* stepped onto dry land. We're told, "Once safely on shore, we found out that the island was called Malta. The islanders showed us unusual kindness. They built a fire and welcomed us all because it was raining and cold" (Acts 28:1–2).

What sweet words those are: *safely onshore*. Can you imagine going through such an ordeal, wondering whether you would escape with your life, and then feeling that moist sand under your feet? Having concerned strangers rush to greet you with blankets and dry clothes? Warming yourself near the blazing fire the hospitable natives have built for you on the beach?

This place wasn't heaven, but it must have felt like it after all Paul and his shipmates had endured. They had landed on an island that we still know today as Malta, located about fifty miles south of Italy, just below Sicily, and roughly two hundred miles from the northeast coast of Africa. If you look at a map of Malta, you can see just how far off course Paul's ship had strayed! I'm sure that, gathering around the fire, all the survivors were just grateful to be on dry land again despite being so far from their destination.

To be received so warmly by the islanders must have been a welcome relief. Although these people didn't know Paul and the other passengers, they would have been well acquainted with the sea and its seasonal storms. The hospitality of the Maltese reminds us to remain vigilant to meet the needs of others who have just come through a storm. In those moments we can pass along the kindnesses we've received when trying to get back on our feet.

We can also celebrate with the people who have helped us through our storms and supported us with their prayers, provision, and positivity. Remember, those who prayed with us in the drought deserve to dance with us in the rain!

I'm guessing that as all 276 passengers looked around that beach at one another, they shared a bond of jubilant camaraderie, much like soldiers coming through a battle. They had all suffered the same terrifying conditions together, and they had now survived and reached dry land—without losing a single life, just as Paul had announced after being told by God.

They were all safely onshore.

ROCK SOLID

Some Christians spend their lives working so hard to make it to the shore of their own expectations. Their struggles with "if only" living aren't focused on their material possessions and accomplishments but on their ministry success and spiritual development. They've simply transferred their comparative, competitive mind-set to the number of hours they volunteer at church, the number of people who attend the Bible study they're leading, or the length of time they spend in prayer and fasting each month.

Again, these are all wonderful spiritual practices when done for the right reason—not because we have to in order to be good Christians but because we want to out of loving worship and sacrificial service to God. He wants our hearts, not our attempts to earn his favor. The essence of grace means we can never earn forgiveness for our sins and the righteousness required for a relationship with the perfect, holy God. And we don't have to! Christ's death on the cross paid the debt we could never pay no matter how hard we tried.

So quit striving, my friend! You've already made it to shore. If you're exhausted, rest in Jesus.

In Christ you have already been forgiven, washed clean, and restored to relationship with your loving Father. The most powerful people on the planet are not the ones with riches, armies, or millions of social-media followers. The most powerful people on the planet are those set free by the blood of the Lamb, Jesus Christ! These are the people who have spiritually and prophetically made it safely to the shores of eternity.

You've made it not because you have perfectly held on to God but because God has perfectly held on to you.

You've made it not because your faith is so efficient but because his grace is always sufficient.

You've made it not because of what you've done but because of what Jesus has already done on the cross.

There's nothing you or I can do to earn God's love, favor, and mercy. The Bible tells us, "All of us have become like one who is unclean, and all our righteous acts are like filthy rags; we all shrivel up like a leaf, and like the wind our sins sweep us away" (Isaiah 64:6). We're also assured, "By grace you have been saved, through faith—and this is not from yourselves, it is the gift of God—not by works, so that no one can boast" (Ephesians 2:8–9).

God's Word could not be clearer. We are saved by grace and through faith, not by our own strength. There's nothing we can do to save ourselves. God gives us salvation as a free gift! This way no one can make it a competition to be superspiritual and self-righteous, which was the old way under the Judaic law. Many religious leaders and legalists would focus on obeying the law but ignore what was going on inside their hearts. Jesus denounced them as hypocrites, snakes, and vipers (see Matthew 23)—enemies of God because of their pride, arrogance, and judgment of others. Not who anyone would want to be!

Striving to live a good life, working to look like the perfect Christian, fighting to become a better person—none of these will get you to heaven. Jesus is your one and only ticket. He said, "I am the way and the truth and the life. No one comes to the Father except through me" (John 14:6). This should bring you even more relief and joy than those shipwrecked passengers felt when they landed on Malta! Jesus is the Solid Rock who never lets you down.

THERE'S ONLY ONE

So why do we still struggle sometimes even after we've been saved? I believe it comes from the tension of living between earth and heaven. We are in the process of being transformed into Christ's likeness yet still are in a mortal body. We've been saved, but God loves us and wants us to grow and become more and more like Jesus.

When you've been through a shipwreck, it can be hard to stand on the shore again. Even though you know you're on solid ground, your body may still sway and lurch with motion sickness as it did while tossed on deck during the storm. You may end up not trusting your senses—wondering when the next storm will hit, where the next disaster will come from, or how the other shoe will drop.

In Christ, however, you can submit the aftereffects of any trauma into his care. He will steady you as you adjust to having the ground beneath your feet again. He will lift you if you fall. He will let you rest on his shoulder and catch your breath. Through the sacrifice of Jesus, you have made it to shore.

Your battle is over.

Your debt is paid.

Your sins are forgiven.

Your life has purpose and meaning.

Your home in heaven awaits you after your time on earth.

You are safely onshore.

So any time you're asked why you're now able to remain calm in a crisis or not go crazy in a catastrophe, you can answer, "Because I'm already safely onshore!" And if you're asked, "How did you make it? What kept you going?" you know the answer and can throw out the same lifeline of grace that saved your soul.

There's only one explanation for how you survived the storm.

There's only one way you got out of the pit.

There's only one key that freed you from your prison.

There's only one reason you're standing today.

God, only God! *Only through the blood of Jesus Christ.*

And you continue to walk by faith each and every day. You have made it by the strength of the Father, the grace of the Son, and the anointing of the Holy Spirit. You may be exhausted, famished, and drenched, but you made it. You may be scared, scarred, and soaked, but you made it. You may be wet, weary, and worn out, but you still made it.

Once you're safely on the shore of salvation, nothing can separate you from God—*nothing*! Not your fears or insecurities. Not your divorce or bankruptcy. Not your disease or injury. Not your addiction or abuse. Not your failed relationships or lost opportunities. When God says *nothing*, he means *not one single thing*! Paul wrote to the church at Rome, "No power in the sky above or in the earth below—indeed, nothing in all creation will ever be able to separate us from the love of God that is revealed in Christ Jesus our Lord" (Romans 8:39, NLT).

> ## It's time to warm yourself by the fire of the Spirit burning within you.

It's time to warm yourself by the fire of the Spirit burning within you. It's time to take a moment to catch your breath before resuming your journey to Rome. It's time to bask in the grace that God has so generously bestowed upon you. It's time to look around at all the other people who are making this journey with you. It's time to look how far you've come before continuing to go the distance.

You endured the storm.

You raised your anchor.

You cut the rope and let go of the lifeboat.

You trusted God for the impossible as your ship sank.

You held tight to the lifeline of grace.

And you set your feet safely onshore.

In Christ you made it!

There is no safer place than with Jesus. He is shelter and solace, comfort and comforter. "For in him we live and move and have our being" (Acts 17:28). Like Paul, you can now say,

I've learned by now to be quite content whatever my circumstances.

I'm just as happy with little as with much, with much as with little.

I've found the recipe for being happy whether full or hungry, hands full or hands empty. Whatever I have, wherever I am, I can make it through anything in the One who makes me who I am. (Philippians 4:11–13, MSG)

You can do all things through Christ, who strengthens you!

SHAKE FREE . . . FROM "IF ONLY" LIVING

As with the previous chapters, the following questions are designed to help you reflect on where you are on your journey of faith and what you need in order to grow closer to God. Spend a few minutes reflecting on each one, asking God's Spirit to reveal ways you can experience the fullness of being safely onshore through the love of Jesus Christ.

1. How much do you struggle with focusing on the future instead of where you are now? What are you looking forward to that often prevents you from seeing what you currently have? What impact does this looking ahead have on your relationship with God?

2. On a scale of one to ten, with one being almost never and ten being most of the time, how frequently do you struggle with an "if only" attitude? How do you usually respond when you become aware of this conditional way of living? How do you wish you would respond? Why?

3. Complete the following statement: I would be happier and more content in my life if only _____

_____.

_____

Jesus, you and you alone are the reason that I am safely onshore. I can never thank you enough for dying on the cross so I can be forgiven and have eternal life. Forgive me for the times I overlook the many blessings I've been given and look ahead to some elusive future event or condition. I repent of the ways I let pride creep in and the times when I want to take credit for all you've done for me. Give me strength not to compare and compete with those around me, especially in the spiritual practices that I want to exercise to be closer to you, Lord. I know it's only by grace that I'm saved. Keep me humble so I can point others to you as the source of all I have. I praise your holy name and give you all that I am! Nothing can separate me from your love. Amen.

10

If You Survived the Storm, You Can Shake the Snake

Snakes. Why'd it have to be snakes?

—Indiana Jones, *Raiders of the Lost Ark*

When our kids were older teenagers, they went through a phase of loving scary movies. They told me they liked the adrenaline rush and the comfort of knowing that the alien/serial killer/clown would be defeated in the end. Never mind that the stories weren't realistic and the acting wasn't very compelling. "It doesn't matter, Dad," my son, Nathan, tried to explain to me. "We like these kinds of movies for the same reason we love riding roller coasters at amusement parks: the sheer thrill of it within a giant safety net. It's just a movie; it's just a ride."

I tried watching a few of their favorites with them, and I don't recommend this genre—for lots of reasons! Even after watching only a few scary movies, I quickly saw the formula. In addition to the creepy setting and the unbelievably oblivious characters, after the chase scenes and the part where the vulnerable young woman goes into the woods/basement/barn where she's been warned not to go, each film has a "Gotcha!" ending—a moment when you think it's over but it isn't.

These heart-stopping surprises usually occur after a dramatic showdown, with the villain seemingly defeated. Just when you think it is safe and the battle is over—bam!—the bad guy/zombie/hockey player comes at you again, one final time. It's like the last hill on the roller coaster ride that's guaranteed to take your breath away right at the end of the ride.

Maybe one of the reasons I don't enjoy these movies, and particularly this kind of false ending, stems from having lived long enough to experience too many "Gotcha!" moments that were real. Those times when you can't believe a bad day just got worse or an uncomfortable situation becomes a full-blown crisis. When a minor injury turns into major surgery. When a disagreement with your spouse leads to a much harder conversation in a courtroom. When an overdue bill crashes into your credit report.

Such experiences often leave us reeling with even more pain, anger, and grief than before. We may even feel foolish for having believed that things were getting better. And that may be the hardest part—that sense of renewed hope, like a tender sprout bursting through the hard ground of our desperate circumstances, suddenly being crushed by one last unexpected blow.

I've certainly experienced my share of those. Times when the church that I knew God called me to plant never took root. Seasons when moving into a new neighborhood became a battle against prejudice as eggs, garbage, and racial slurs were thrown at us. Days when I already felt lonely and exhausted but kept my commitment to minister to other parts of the world, only to be stranded in airports with grounded flights. And I know my experiences are minor compared with what so many suffering people endure in our world today.

But even when the ache within us is amplified, even when events leave us hoarse from crying out to God, even when we make it through the valley, only to stumble into one last pothole, we must never give up. Especially in these bottom-of-the-barrel moments, we must trust the Lord to pick us up again and sustain us. Like Paul landing in Malta, only to face one more unexpected blow, we must learn to shake it off.

HANGING FROM HIS HAND

Of all the dramatic moments that occurred over the course of Paul's journey to Rome, there's one that still blows my mind. This part of the story stops me in my tracks!

> Paul gathered a pile of brushwood and, as he put it on the fire, a viper, driven out by the heat, fastened itself on his hand. When the islanders saw the snake hanging from his hand, they said to each other, "This man must be a murderer; for though he escaped from the sea, the goddess Justice has not allowed him to live." But Paul shook the snake off into the fire and suffered no ill effects. (Acts 28:3–5)

Now, you have to admit, the Bible is filled with strange, amazing, miraculous events. Noah building an ark when there wasn't a cloud in the sky, chosen by God to be one of the only survivors, along with his family and a boatful of animals, of the horrendous flood that destroyed the rest of mankind. Moses parting the Red Sea for the people of Israel to escape Pharaoh's soldiers on the way out of Egypt. Daniel remaining unharmed in the den of lions that his Babylonian captors assumed would kill him. The stories of Rahab's scarlet thread and the widow's jar of oil. And that's just scratching the surface of the Old Testament!

In the New Testament we find just as many incredible incidents. Moments when water becomes wine, when a few loaves and fish feed thousands of people, when the lame, blind, or even dead instantly walk, see, or return to life. And, of course, there's the resurrection of the One who performed those miracles, Jesus Christ!

In comparison with those events, Paul's encounter with this viper may seem rather small. Nonetheless, I still consider this scene where Paul is bitten by a snake—*after* he's arrested without cause, *after* he's a prisoner on a ship, *after* he's weathered the storm of all storms, *after* he's survived a shipwreck and made it to Malta—my favorite "Gotcha!" moment in the Bible. The first time I read it, I did not see this twist coming.

I mean, are you kidding me? Just imagine Paul's face. His body was drenched. He was cold and exhausted. He'd just survived a shipwreck and washed up onshore. And then, out of the fire—without any warning—a snake struck. Yes, a snake! It "fastened itself on his hand" (verse 3) and was hanging from it! Can you imagine that scene? Unfortunately, I can! I'm with Indiana Jones when it comes to snakes—I don't like 'em and would rather avoid 'em at all costs.

But Paul apparently didn't even flinch!

He just shook it off.

With no ill effects.

ALL AT ONCE

After Paul endured and persevered through one hardship after another, we expect him—just as we expect for ourselves—to finally come out the other side. When we've survived a season of Job-like loss and grief, we want to believe that we deserve to get to a place where life gets better. I suspect that's a big part of why all human beings across all cultures love stories. Whether true stories from the past or fictional stories set in the future, these tales fundamentally have a beginning, a middle, and an end.

I recall from my literature classes that tragedy and comedy, the two primary forms of drama, both begin with a problem, conflict, or disruption. Tragedy then follows the main character's descent into loss and ends (sometimes) with a lesson learned or wisdom gained. Comedy, on the other hand, includes a descent into hardship before there's a reversal and everyone lives happily ever after. Forgive me for the lecture, but I tell you this to point out the way our human expectations are formed concerning the stories of our lives.

After so much hardship and trauma, after one domino of destruction topples into another for a chain reaction of radical reduction, we expect to hit rock bottom. And after hitting rock bottom, we have nowhere to go but up! We want things to get better and may think we deserve for them to improve.

Perhaps this explains why the story of Job's life is so powerful. He suffered one devastating tragedy after another: losing his animals, his income, his servants, and his children. And that's just in the first chapter! But even after such catastrophes, we're told Job chose not to give up on God:

> At this, Job got up and tore his robe and shaved his head. Then he fell
> to the ground in worship and said:
>
>> "Naked I came from my mother's womb,
>>   and naked I will depart.
>> The LORD gave and the LORD has taken away;
>>   may the name of the LORD be praised."
>
> In all this, Job did not sin by charging God with wrongdoing. (1:20–22)

Now, losing your job, your financial savings, your car, or your house delivers a major blow that would jolt any of us. But losing them *all at once*—and then facing the loss of your *children*—is simply staggering!

This makes Job's response so amazing, because even after having everything he loved and valued stripped away, he still didn't feel sorry for himself. He didn't become a victim. He didn't give up hope and sink into despair. He didn't abandon his faith and his belief in the goodness of God.

Later, after he began talking with his wife and friends, who each encouraged him to curse God and give in to death, Job declared, "Though [God] slay me, yet will I hope in him. . . . Indeed, this will turn out for my deliverance" (13:15–16).

What Job did do was express the volcanic emotions in his heart while still choosing to trust in God. He made it clear that even if God killed him, he would still hope in the Lord! Job refused to let his circumstances, no matter how dire they were, rob him of hope. He knew that without hope, our souls despair. And when we despair, we give up—on trying, on living, on God.

If you had nothing left in your life, would you still keep your spark of hope alive? Hope fuels the engine of our faith. It allows us to get up and step forward after being knocked down again and again and again. We're told, "Faith is confidence in what we hope for and assurance about what we do not see" (Hebrews 11:1).

If everything is going well, it's easy to keep things status quo with God. When your bills are paid, your job is sound, your kids are healthy, and your marriage is happy, it's easy to praise God and thank him for his many blessings. It's easy to give him tithes and offerings and participate in your small group's Bible study. It's easy to pray and read the Bible and console others going through hard times.

But when you're the one going through hard times, it's no longer so easy to keep the faith. Nothing seems to matter once you feel as though you've lost everything, so why bother? When a loved one dies, you may not feel like praising God or notice the blessings that remain in your life. When you're out of work for months and watching your bank account dwindle down to single digits, you might struggle to trust God to provide that job you need. When you're battling depression and can't seem to shake the weight of sadness crushing your soul, you may wonder why God seems so far away.

In those moments, though, when the viper of the unexpected leaps out of the fire to bite you, you have to shake it off. No matter what else you've been through or how many losses you've suffered, you can't let the sting of the temporary setback become the poison of hopelessness. You can't give up the fight! You simply have to shake it off.

DON'T PANIC

Just as we noticed the significance of what Job did not do when the worst happened to him, let's also note what Paul did not do when that snake latched on to him. He didn't panic or immediately give up and resign himself to death. He didn't denounce God and embrace a cynical view of a world where snakes jump out of fires to bite shipwreck-surviving prisoners. He didn't create drama and demand to be the center of attention among those around him. He didn't embrace the snake or tolerate it.

Paul just shook it off!

Notice, too, how the islanders responded to Paul's plight: "This man must be a murderer; for though he escaped from the sea, the goddess Justice has not allowed him to live" (Acts 28:4). They assumed the worst: that Paul had to be a terrible person because this terrible thing was happening to him right after another terrible thing. They judged the stranger in their midst based on their worldviews and perceptions of life. Their notion of justice was a goddess who controlled events to reward those she favored and punish those who were criminals. Similar to Job's so-called friends, they wanted to believe that Paul had somehow brought this on himself.

We may be tempted to do the same. If only we had read the Bible and prayed more, then this bad break wouldn't have happened. If only we weren't such bad people, then maybe we wouldn't go through the trials that seem to trail us. If only we had done this or not done that, then maybe our lives would be different. But that's not accurate! Such logic is human-centric, not God-centric. When we place ourselves at the center of our lives, we will be tempted to think we can control what happens to us. But the truth is that God is always in control, even when we don't understand why he allows certain things to happen—like snakes jumping out to bite us! He remains present for us and has prepared us to know what to do when those poisonous moments try to get under our skin. His Spirit gives us the power to shake off what may have been intended to harm us.

There's no need to panic, because God is still in control!

SHAKE, SHAKE, SHAKE

When one of life's "Gotcha!" moments leaps out at you, especially when you're already struggling to get back on your feet, you must trust God to give you the strength to shake it off. Maybe you would not have been able to shake free of this thing so quickly five years ago, three months ago, or even yesterday. Back then you might have panicked, but today, my friend, you have what it takes to shake the snake and send it slinking back into the fiery pit from which it came!

Why can you shake it off now when you couldn't before? Because you're not the person you used to be. You've been through a storm. You've survived a shipwreck. You've made it to shore. You've already been through circumstances that at one time you could never have imagined surviving. By the grace of God and the power of his Spirit, you have made it to where you are right now. And through it all, *God was faithful.*

Through it all, God provided.

Through it all, God protected.

Through it all, God promoted.

Through it all, you found out that God causes everything to work together for the good of those who love him and are called according to his purpose for them (see Romans 8:28).

Through it all, you grabbed hold of the promise that if God is for you, there is no one who can be against you (see verse 31).

Through it all, you discovered that nothing can separate you from the love of God (see verses 38–39).

So when the Enemy springs an attack on you, remind yourself of God's truth and not the devil's lies. Learn to say, "You picked the wrong child of God to bite today, Mr. Viper! Because I carry an anointing—a blessing, courage, and strength—that was born out of adversity. My anointing didn't come on a silver platter. It didn't arrive from Amazon.com wrapped in comfort and convenience. My anointing was given to me in the midst of life's storms and was sealed by a shipwreck!"

When your God-given confidence and ability are born out of adversity, grounded in hope, and powered by faith in the living God, you can shake off everything hell may send your way. You are no longer who you used to be. You are not who others say you are. You are not even the person you may think you are!

You are God's precious, beloved child with all the resources of your Father's kingdom at hand. You are a joint heir with Jesus Christ. You are sealed by the Spirit of God, and nothing can separate you from the divine destiny awaiting you in Rome.

We're told, "I have given you authority to trample on snakes and scorpions and to overcome all the power of the enemy; nothing will harm you" (Luke 10:19). And when God says *nothing*, he means *nothing*! In his Word, he also assures us,

> They will fight you, but they will fail.
> For I am with you, and I will take care of you.
> I, the LORD, have spoken! (Jeremiah 1:19, NLT)

Storm survivors are not afraid of snakes.
Shipwreck survivors are not threatened by what comes out of the fire.

Snakebite survivors know to shake off whatever jumps out at them.

All the things that once hurt you, threatened you, scared you, intimidated you, and tried to harm you have now made you stronger. Nothing can happen to you that you cannot shake off with God's power. So don't allow the Enemy to slither his way into your thoughts and poison your dreams. Shake it off! Long before it was Taylor Swift's hit song, it was Paul's way of life.

When problems come, don't overanalyze them—shake them off!

When conflicts arise, don't fear them—shake them off!

When disasters loom, don't lose hope—shake them off!

> ## The Enemy has no hold on you whatsoever.

God has given you an anointing to overcome the Enemy. Your prayers will stop him. Your praise will confuse him. Your peace will paralyze him. Your integrity will disarm him. And your resistance will make him flee.

The Enemy has no hold on you whatsoever. And when he lashes out at you, there's no time to stand and wait for his poison to take effect. You must act fast and be deliberate in your response, which isn't hard because you know what to do: shake it off!

Shake off rejection.

Shake off closed doors.

Shake off negativity.

Shake off failure.

Shake off the past.

Shake off complacency.

Shake off apathy.

Shake off unbelief.

Shake off unforgiveness.

Shake off bitterness.

Shake off fear.

No matter what it is, if it's not of God, shake it off!

SHAKE FREE . . . FROM LIFE'S VIPERS

No one enjoys being blindsided or caught off guard by life's vipers. But through God's power, protection, and provision, you can shake off anything that jumps out at you. Use the following questions to reflect on how to overcome any fears you have of life's many unexpected moments.

1. Are you the kind of person who likes surprises and change, or do you prefer to keep things the same and predictable? When have you most recently seen this tendency demonstrated in your life? How does this disposition affect the way you respond when something unexpected and painful occurs?

2. What are some of the major unexpected events that have shaped your life? In what ways have these events had both positive and negative effects? How have you grown stronger because of these events?

3. Looking back on your life, when have you encountered circumstances or endured a season that shook your faith and made you question your relationship with God? What kept you going through that period? How is your faith stronger because of it?

Heavenly Father, you know all I've been through, and I know you're the only reason I've made it this far. Thank you for protecting me and guiding me through the many twists and turns of my life. I may not know what's around the next curve, but you do, Lord. I trust you to show me the way and illuminate my path. And when vipers jump out at me, help me not to panic but to respond just like Paul and shake it off. When others judge me or label me, give me the strength to ignore them and rely on you. I'm confident that you have anointed me for your purposes and that you will be faithful to complete what you have started in my life. With your continued help and guidance, I'm closer to Rome every day! Lead me on, Lord. Amen.

11

Shipwreck Survivors Surprise the World

Life is never more fun than when you're the underdog competing against the giants.

—Ross Perot

Have you attended any of your high school or college class reunions? I've been to only a couple, and from my limited experience, they're definitely full of surprises. Former classmates don't always turn out to be the people we imagined they would be. Perhaps the student voted "Most Likely to Succeed" ended up as the manager at the local Red Lobster, a fine job but not what everyone expected. On the other hand, the scruffy kid who got bullied as the butt of class jokes may have started a dot-com company right after college and sold it to Google five years later for millions. And the pretty cheerleader with the perfect body? Like the rest of us, she's put on a few pounds, while the "plain Jane" no one asked to prom blossomed into a beautiful person both inside and out.

I've certainly enjoyed surprising my former classmates. The ones who didn't really know me assumed I'd end up working construction or landscaping or some other job that fit their stereotype of Hispanics. And the ones who did know me figured I would end up glued to a computer screen at some engineering firm or government department. None of them imagined I would become a Christian pastor leading America's largest Hispanic evangelical organization. That guidance counselor who advised me to settle for so much less than my potential never dreamed I would be delivering prayers at presidential inaugurations in Washington.

Life is full of surprises.

No Good Reason

As I've shared with you, it hasn't always been easy for me. Plenty of people, both inside and outside the church, have doubted, criticized, and judged me and my ministry. And they still do! When I first started as a pastor, I naively assumed that the larger my church grew and the bigger my platform became, the fewer critics I would have to face. I figured that if my ministry was healthy and growing, I would be valued and appreciated more. Boy, was I wrong!

Though I'm privileged to lead a team of talented, devoted, loyal supporters now and enjoy the amazing support of thousands of people in our country and around the world, I still have plenty of haters throwing shade my way. I think social media may actually fan the angry sparks from these dissenters and naysayers, giving them opportunities—often anonymous—to leave caustic comments and bombastic blah, blah, blah. I rarely read their diatribes anymore, let alone respond, but when I do, I often like to surprise them by agreeing with them.

"You're a terrible preacher, Rodriguez! You talk too fast and your voice gets too loud. And you use too much Spanish," a lurker might write. To which I like to respond, "Guess what, hater1234? You're absolutely right! I know all those things you say might be true. But I also know I'm doing what God has called me to do, and it's not up to me to be the top of the Toastmasters or the leading TED talker. The Lord speaks through me and apparently communicates effectively despite all my flaws and inadequacies. To God be the glory!"

As you might imagine, those haters usually don't write back. They don't know what to do with a shipwreck survivor like me who continues to be used by God again and again. There's no good reason—only a God reason! They don't understand how much God loves to use not the biggest, strongest, or most talented but instead the weak, wobbly, and willing. People like Paul and Moses and David, like Ruth and Esther and Rahab.

People like you and me.

SURPRISE, SURPRISE

When people see God work through one of his underdogs, many don't know how to respond. After their expectations go unmet and their assumptions are challenged, they're thrown for a loop, shocked at the results of someone being infused with God's power. This was certainly the case with the islanders in Malta when Paul and the other shipwrecked survivors landed.

After the Maltese people witnessed the viper jumping out of the woodpile and latching on to Paul's hand, they speculated that he must be a terrible person being punished by their goddess Justice. For them, there was no other explanation for the irony that Paul had survived the shipwreck, only to reach shore so he could be bitten by this viper. This "Gotcha!" moment seemed too conspicuous not to mean something, so they interpreted it through their limited perspective.

When Paul shook the snake off, however, those watching were in for an even greater surprise. "The people expected him to swell up or suddenly fall dead; but after waiting a long time and seeing nothing unusual happen to him, they changed their minds and said he was a god" (Acts 28:6). I can't fault them for what they expected to happen. Many times when a snake bites someone, that person's body swells from the poison and then he dies.

But not this time.

This time God protected Paul and allowed him to shake off the viper and toss it back where it came from. God had not brought Paul all that distance, saving him through that horrendous storm, rescuing him from that terrible shipwreck, just to have him die from a snakebite. Paul knew this as well, and I suspect that's why he remained so calm and just shook it off in the same way you or I might swat a fly.

When you've been chosen and equipped for the purposes of God, you can have confidence that he will get you to Rome. You may take the long route, experience some unexpected detours, get delayed by a storm, and arrive by other means than how you started, but you will get there. And anything that tries to slow you down or block your path is no match for the unrelenting, supernatural power of our almighty God!

The people watching Paul expected him to swell up and die from that snakebite. The people watching you may be expecting you to quit your job, file for divorce, declare bankruptcy, stop pursuing your degree, or give up hope. My friend, they're in for a huge surprise when they look up and see what God is doing in your life! They won't be able to explain how you got promoted instead of fired, how your marriage is stronger than ever despite the gossip, or how you got out of debt, started your own business, or returned to church.

Those focused on earth cannot understand the things of heaven. And I'm not just talking about nonbelievers, sadly enough. Many religious people get upset when God uses the people they have deemed unqualified. Like the Pharisees and scribes in Jesus's day, these self-righteous individuals assume that their expectations about God and what he will or will not do are correct. But the Lord is no respecter of persons and bows to no one. He does things his way and delights in doing the impossible through the most unlikely individuals in order to display his breathtaking glory and conspicuous, supernatural presence.

And sometimes it's not other people who are surprised by what God does as much as the person he's using to do it. We get in our own way, even when it's clear the Lord has called us and is leading us to the Rome he has divinely appointed for us. Even when we already can see the way, we make excuses and ask a lot of questions about how he can possibly do it. Occasionally, we even go so far as to test him to be sure we heard him correctly.

Just like Gideon, we put out a fleece.

YOU TALKIN' TO ME?

Of all the underdogs in the Bible, one of my favorites is Gideon. Not only did he come from the least influential clan in his tribe, but he was also the youngest member of his family (see Judges 6:15). Unlike confident and capable David, the shepherd boy so eager to take on the giant Goliath, Gideon reminds me of the computer nerds I ran with back in school, the Peter Parkers of the Marvel Universe. We kept our heads down and tried not to get noticed, in part because most of us were introverts and felt awkward socially and in part not to attract attention from bullies seeking new targets.

Instead of playing video games, though, Gideon was completing domestic duties when God's messenger showed up and changed this young underdog's life forever:

> The angel of the LORD came and sat down under the oak in Ophrah that belonged to Joash the Abiezrite, where his son Gideon was threshing wheat in a winepress to keep it from the Midianites. When the angel of the LORD appeared to Gideon, he said, "The LORD is with you, mighty warrior."
>
> "Pardon me, my lord," Gideon replied, "but if the LORD is with us, why has all this happened to us? Where are all his wonders that our ancestors told us about when they said, 'Did not the LORD bring us up out of Egypt?' But now the LORD has abandoned us and given us into the hand of Midian."

The LORD turned to him and said, "Go in the strength you have and save Israel out of Midian's hand. Am I not sending you?"

"Pardon me, my lord," Gideon replied, "but how can I save Israel? My clan is the weakest in Manasseh, and I am the least in my family."

The LORD answered, "I will be with you, and you will strike down all the Midianites, leaving none alive." (verses 11–16)

This scene always cracks me up! There's Gideon, minding his own business and doing a domestic job that the women in his household usually performed. He's threshing wheat, separating the grain from the husks, in a winepress using a tool designed to crush grapes. I offer this as a clever improvisation that further proves Gideon's engineering intellect. He was an inventor, not a fighter.

So Gideon's doing his thing with the wheat when this angel of the Lord shows up and greets him as a "mighty warrior" (verse 12). Right away Gideon knows something's up. Being addressed as a warrior meant the speaker was either ignorant of Gideon's identity or aware and mocking him for it. It would be like someone meeting me for the first time and mistaking me for wrestlers John Cena or Dwayne Johnson, The Rock!

Gideon wasn't buying it. He basically said, "Uh, if God is with me and the other Israelites, why are the Midianites occupying our land and trampling all over us? Where's the God of the past who did all those amazing things to deliver us from Egypt? If God is with us, why is he letting Midian destroy us?" The angel was apparently just greeting Gideon in his usual manner, similar to what we see in other angelic encounters—for instance, when Gabriel visited Mary (see Luke 1:28). But Gideon took the angel's greeting literally and went off!

Prior to this scene, we're told that the Hebrew people had fallen away from the Lord "yet again" (Judges 6:1, MSG). Now, you'd think that after all the dramatic events that led to their escape from four hundred years of slavery in

Egypt—the plagues, the parting of the Red Sea, God's provision of food and water, not to mention their arrival in the Promised Land of Canaan—the Jewish people would have remained eternally grateful and unwaveringly faithful.

This was not the case. As soon as they got unpacked and settled into Canaan, their hearts started wandering. All kinds of intriguing pagan gods, remnants of previous inhabitants, littered the area—gods dealing with weather, fertility, battle, you name it. So the Israelites drifted further and further away from the God who loved them so much, until he finally allowed the marauding Midianites to conquer his chosen people—just so he could get their attention back. By the time the angel showed up with his message for Gideon, once again the people of Israel had started to cry out for God to save them. God heard their cries and, because he's so loving and faithful, decided it was time to rescue them.

But only on his terms, his way.

Which brings us back to the angel's response to Gideon, something that must have really shocked him. "That's why I'm here. *You're* going to save your people from the Midianites! God is sending *you*."

This bold announcement apparently seemed just as crazy to Gideon as when the angel said the Lord was with him. "Uh, excuse me, but I'm the least likely guy to save Israel! Not only is my clan the weakest, but I'm also the youngest and scrawniest in my family. How am *I* supposed to save anybody?"

And I just love the Lord's reply. He told Gideon, "I will be with you, and you will be able to do what I'm telling you is gonna happen!"

God's response was a declaration, not an explanation.

It was a statement, not a question.

It was a fact, not a fantasy.

It was the future, not the past.

So often we get hung up on asking God how he can possibly do what he says he's going to do, because we can't see or understand it. We get blinded by human logic and the limitations of the natural world as we know them. We see only horizontally, but God sees horizontally, vertically, and upside down! He dwells above and beyond our dimensions of space and time. "Humanly speaking, it is impossible. But with God everything is possible" (Matthew 19:26, NLT).

You don't have to understand how he will bring about what he has chosen for you to do; you just have to do it. Don't surmise anything when you can surprise everyone!

SEAL THE DEAL

Gideon's response implies that he saw himself not as a mighty warrior but rather as a nerd, runt, wallflower—someone used to doing household chores in a winepress, not charging into battle with a sword. Gideon saw no superhero hiding underneath his dusty robe.

So what did Gideon do, not just once, but repeatedly? He stalled and kept asking God, "Are you sure about this? You really think I can do this thing you've told me to do?" And even as the Lord continued to reassure him, Gideon took it a step further and laid out the fleeces for which he has become famous:

> Gideon said to God, "If you will save Israel by my hand as you have promised—look, I will place a wool fleece on the threshing floor. If there is dew only on the fleece and all the ground is dry, then I will know that you will save Israel by my hand, as you said." And that is what happened. Gideon rose early the next day; he squeezed the fleece and wrung out the dew—a bowlful of water.
>
> Then Gideon said to God, "Do not be angry with me. Let me make just one more request. Allow me one more test with the fleece,

but this time make the fleece dry and let the ground be covered with dew." That night God did so. Only the fleece was dry; all the ground was covered with dew. (Judges 6:36–40)

Not only did Gideon set out his little confirmation test for God, but when he got positive results, he had to flip it in order to be sure! I'm telling you, Gideon was an engineer at heart! Before risking all he had by stepping out in faith and leading his people in battle to defeat the Midianites—which is exactly what he went on to do (see Judges 7)—Gideon wanted to be as sure as he could be. And being the kind, patient God that he is, the Lord humored him and confirmed his tests, wetting the fleece one morning and keeping it dry the next.

Have you ever asked God for this kind of confirmation? Do you ever stall and drag your feet as Gideon did, wondering why God would pick someone like you? Someone so unqualified, someone who doesn't like to lead or speak in public, someone who doesn't have a degree or come from the richest family?

> ## You have the same warrior spirit inside you that the angel recognized in Gideon.

Why is it so hard for you to accept that God would never have called you if he hadn't already equipped you? You've been through the storms, the shipwrecks, and the snakebites of life. He has blessed and prepared you, whether you feel it all the time or not. Knowing how far he has already brought you, do you really need to doubt you'll get to Rome?

So think twice before you question God or ask for confirmation. I'm not here to debate the theology of fleeces, but I am interested in your motives when you try to test God rather than get on with the journey on which he is obviously leading you. Seeing how far he has brought you, why should you be surprised at what he is now about to do? You are more than a conqueror for a reason. You have the same warrior spirit inside you that the angel recognized in Gideon. God says,

> For I am about to do something new.
>   See, I have already begun! Do you not see it?
> I will make a pathway through the wilderness.
>   I will create rivers in the dry wasteland. (Isaiah 43:19, NLT)

SURPRISE PARTY

No matter how you may feel, you have God's seal. So expect to surprise those around you. Expect to surprise those who said, "You can't do that! You'll never make it! You're not strong enough!"

Expect to surprise those around you waiting on you to swell up and die.

Expect to surprise those who assumed you'd give up your faith.

Expect to surprise everyone who doubted that you have what it takes.

No worries! God always has what it takes, and he has chosen you to demonstrate his grace, love, and mercy. Your life is a masterpiece of his miracles, a testament to his triumphs, and a prism of his power. Others will marvel as they see you not only live but thrive.

Your life is God's surprise party to the world around you. And there's much to celebrate! You are so close to Rome right now. Snakebites are merely speed bumps on your journey. Don't let others' expectations erode your belief in what God wants to do in you. They will often be shocked by your life, but you should not be. You know God loves you and has created you for a specific purpose. There's no doubt he's anointed you with the gift of his Holy Spirit inside you. There's no doubt you would never have made it this far without God at work in your life. You have all you need to fulfill your divine potential. Let God surprise everyone around you with all that he wants to accomplish through your life!

SHAKE FREE . . . FROM OTHERS' EXPECTATIONS

We all struggle at times with wanting to please others by living up to their expectations. Similarly, we may sometimes struggle because of the limitations others want to impose on us. They see us through human eyes, but God sees us for who we really are and for all that he made us to be. Let the following questions help you reflect on ways you can trust God to surprise those around you, even if you end up surprised as well.

1. Do you think of yourself as a competitive person? How often do you compare yourself with others around you? Do you think of yourself as an underdog in life? Why or why not?

2. How does your awareness of what other people expect of you influence your willingness to step out in faith? Can you think of a time this has happened recently?

3. When have you seen God work in your life in a way that left you, as well as others, surprised by the outcome? How did you feel going through that experience? How does that experience, and others similar to it, strengthen your faith in God's plan for you right now?

4. When have you, like Gideon, set out a fleece for confirmation of God's calling on your life? What were the results? How often do you still long to have certainty about what you know God has called you to do? How do you handle any lingering doubts or difficulties?

Dear God, I sometimes struggle to see myself through your eyes and to be the person you've created and called me to be. Give me strength to ignore others' criticism and harsh judgments so that I may focus instead on the truth of who you are and what you have said in your Word. Forgive me, Lord, when I drag my feet in obeying your call or when I lay out a fleece for confirmation. Empower me with the boldness of Paul when he shook off that viper so that I, too, may surprise those around me. And with every triumph and victory in my life, I want you to be exalted and glorified! You are the reason I can do the impossible, and nothing surprises you. I praise you for sustaining me on this journey and for the joy of reaching Rome soon! Amen.

12

Stronger from the Struggle

If we see only the problems, we will be defeated; but if we see the possibilities in the problems, we can have victory.

—Warren Wiersbe,
The Bumps Are What You Climb On

I t takes one to know one." Visiting a faith-based recovery group for people addicted to drugs and alcohol, I had just asked the founder of this ministry why he thought his organization had grown so quickly. What had begun for him as a small-group Bible study in a church basement two years earlier had blossomed into a nonprofit maxing out a converted warehouse in the downtown of a major midwestern city. His ministry was running not only support groups but also a shelter, a soup kitchen, and job training for those in recovery.

"Obviously, God has blessed us," said the organization's founder, a bearded and tatted Latino in his midthirties who might seem imposing if not for the warmth behind his brown eyes and constant smile. "But I think it helps that I've faced what most of our participants are facing. I was hooked by thirteen and dealing by fifteen. It's only by the grace of God that I got arrested and found Jesus before it was too late. I've been clean and sober now for more than fifteen years. When God called me to start this, I didn't think I was cut out for it. And I still think that most days. But he's with me every step of the way."

This brother's story has become familiar to me. I see it time and again: thriving ministries birthed in the desolation of people's struggles. Led by God's

Spirit as they love and serve those in need, these vibrant kingdom builders have allowed their wounds to become God's wonder. They have seen God transform the area where the Enemy assaulted them into a conduit of his grace. Because they experienced the Lord's power, overcame the Enemy, and allowed God to work through what was once a weakness, many others are now finding comfort, peace, and healing.

BRIDGE OF MERCY

It's the same kind of miraculous transformation I see in Annie Lobert. Like so many young women, Annie grew up looking in all the wrong places for the love she didn't get at home. This search led her into the dark alleys of prostitution and sex trafficking in Las Vegas. She grew dependent on drugs and alcohol to numb her pain and became reliant on money to fuel her habits, which led to years of abuse by various violent, controlling men. After being diagnosed and treated for cancer, Annie reached rock bottom and came close to taking her own life with a drug overdose.

That's when she finally surrendered to the love of the Lord Jesus. Over the years, Annie had experienced God's pursuit of her heart but could never bring herself to accept his invitation—until she had nowhere to turn. Slowly but tenderly, the Lord worked in Annie's life to bring her healing at every level: physically, emotionally, spiritually. She discovered that only God can restore people so that life's storms and scars no longer define them. Only he can reshape our mistakes and messes into his masterpiece of mercy.

Once she experienced God's power, love, and healing, Annie felt led to share the good news with others ensnared in the sex industry. Like my new friend leading the urban recovery organization, Annie planted seeds of grace that soon grew into a grassroots movement, which then blossomed into an international nonprofit ministry. With a vision to hook, give hope to, heal, and help the men and women caught in the sex trade industry, Hookers for Jesus (www.hookersforjesus.net), founded by Annie in 2005, continues to rescue, restore, and rehabilitate thousands of lives.

Today Annie shares her dramatic story, which she chronicled in her book, *Fallen: Out of the Sex Industry and into the Arms of the Savior,* and uses it to offer hope to those who feel hopeless. So many lives changed, hearts healed, and souls saved, all because one woman let God transform her pain into a perfect prism for shining his light into the world's darkness. The area of her life where the Enemy tried to shame and claim her instead became a springboard for God's grace and a bridge of mercy for so many others.

Shipwreck survivors embrace the truth that the area the Enemy attacks the most is the same area God will use the most for his glory!

VENOM INTO VICTORY

Paul's entire life reflects this same vital truth. While he had once been so zealous about keeping Jewish religious laws, after he met Jesus on the road to Damascus in a dramatic showdown, Paul became even more passionate about sharing the liberating grace of God's love and mercy through Jesus Christ. Paul went from persecuting believers to recruiting them for the revolution of grace led by his Lord and Savior.

Paul's passion for evangelism reminds us of his motive for making this most incredible of journeys to Rome. Faithful to God's voice and the Spirit's guidance, Paul knew that what his enemies intended for his demise would become a divine destination. As we saw back at the beginning of his voyage, on the surface it appeared that Paul was going to Rome to face criminal charges before the court after being arrested in Jerusalem. From an eternal perspective, though, God was working to put Paul in place as a pillar for the church God wanted to grow there.

This same paradox—Paul's weakness becoming God's strength—got spotlighted once again after Paul landed on Malta following the shipwreck. Who can forget that dramatic "Gotcha!" on the beach when the viper fastened itself to Paul's hand! What happened next was also remarkable, especially one small detail:

> There was an estate nearby that belonged to Publius, the chief official of the island. He welcomed us to his home and showed us generous hospitality for three days. His father was sick in bed, suffering from fever and dysentery. Paul went in to see him and, after prayer, placed his hands on him and healed him. When this had happened, the rest of the sick on the island came and were cured. They honored us in many ways; and when we were ready to sail, they furnished us with the supplies we needed. (Acts 28:7–10)

Did you notice that little detail? *Paul used the same hand the snake had attacked to heal the sick!* The hand that recently had a viper dangling from it was the same one Paul used to heal Publius's father and all the sick on the island of Malta. Talk about a total turnaround!

The islanders expected Paul to swell up and die, but instead they saw him remain healthy and heal others who were sick. Based on what they saw and understood from a human perspective, Paul should have collapsed, ballooned as the poison circulated, and died. But God was protecting Paul. He not only saved him from the venom but also transformed the wound site into an instrument of victory.

You see, so often the Enemy attacks the areas God wants to use for his glory. We endure the battle and suffer through the wounds, at times wondering whether we'll make it out alive. Then as we see God provide for, protect, and empower us, we realize we're going to make it to shore, and we shake off any snake that strikes. Yes, we now believe we're going to make it to Rome, but what we don't always realize is that God will also redeem our suffering so that others may know him.

If the Enemy is attacking you, it's because God is about to use you.

If the Enemy is attacking your life, it's because God is working in you.

If the Enemy is attacking your weakness, it's because you're about to display God's strength.

If the Enemy is attacking you right now, it's because you're so close to arriving in Rome!

So close!

WHAT A SHAME

Even after you've endured the storm and shaken off the snake, you may still resist allowing God to use you and your weaknesses. You may say you're willing, but, like Gideon, you still make excuses or lay out endless fleeces. In these instances, we often are facing one of the Enemy's deadliest weapons—a last-resort, slow-acting poison that's summed up by the word *shame.*

Before I elaborate on the remedy for shame, let me distinguish it from a few other words it often attaches itself to, such as *guilt* and *conviction* and *conscience.* Shame differs from these other words because it causes you to fixate on yourself and maintain a human—what I like to call horizontal—perspective. Shame lingers on what you've done or not done, said or not said, haunting your mind and heart with images from the past.

Before Adam and Eve blew it and sinned in the garden, "the man and his wife were both naked, but they felt no shame" (Genesis 2:25, NLT). This is a sharp contrast to when they messed up and saw their nakedness, sewed fig leaves to cover themselves, and hid from God (see Genesis 3). After they succumbed to the devil's temptation, Adam and Eve suffered not just because of their awareness of having disobeyed God but also because of how they felt about their disobedience.

I suspect we've been struggling with the same distinction ever since. When we become aware of our sin, we know we have disobeyed God and need forgiveness. His Word tells us, "If we confess our sins, he is faithful and just and will forgive us our sins and purify us from all unrighteousness" (1 John 1:9). This is the gift of grace purchased by Christ's death on the cross.

The problem, as I see it, occurs when we know we're forgiven but sometimes don't *feel* as though we're forgiven. This is shame territory. The Enemy then fans the flame of these falsely based feelings to keep us quiet and passive. He hopes he can amp up the shame feelings enough so that we're unwilling to tell others our stories and share what God has done. "After all," the Enemy says to us, "why would anyone believe you anyway? You're just a prostitute. A druggie. An addict. A liar. An adulterer." Or, "You don't read your Bible enough. You are a loser at loving people. You don't tithe. You have that hidden sin that you can't lick—you hypocrite!" On and on his list of accusations flicker at us, like the snake's tongue seeking to poison our hearts.

But the Enemy has no power against us! Once we have been forgiven through the blood of Jesus shed on the cross, we are no longer who we once were. "But now [God] has reconciled you by Christ's physical body through death to present you holy in his sight, without blemish and free from accusation" (Colossians 1:22). Even after we know this is true and have been following Jesus for years, we may still struggle with forgiving ourselves and seeing ourselves as God sees us.

And this struggle is where the Enemy latches on and tries to poison us. The Bible tells us, "Your enemy the devil prowls around like a roaring lion looking for someone to devour" (1 Peter 5:8). We're also told the devil is the accuser (see Revelation 12:10), attempting to undermine our relationship with God by hurling condemnation. So even though we have God's Spirit living in us and have experienced God's amazing power in our lives, the Enemy may still be attacking us by trying to shame us over the past.

It's crucial to look at the difference between shame, which wraps you in embarrassment and inadequacy, and a healthy conscience, which the Spirit uses to convict you to repent, because if you recognize the difference, it can help you experience healing as you totally yield all areas of your life—even those you consider your worst—to God for his glory. The Enemy doesn't want you doing anything that will bring God glory and further his kingdom. The last thing the Enemy wants is for the place he's attacked to become the foundation of ministry and healing for others!

> ## The Enemy doesn't want you doing anything that will bring God glory and further his kingdom.

The devil does not want you to start that Bible study for other divorced people.

The devil does not want you sharing your story and praying with the friend addicted to porn.

The devil does not want you to help others examine their finances and get out of debt.

The devil does not want you speaking at the women's retreat about how God healed your marriage.

The devil does not want you mentoring the new church member struggling to overcome alcoholism.

The devil does not want you using the hand he tried to bite.

But he cannot stop you!

WALKING ON WATER

Because of the power of Jesus's death and resurrection, the devil has already been defeated. The victory is won! The Enemy doesn't get what he wants, no matter how much he tries to shame you. He may have kept you quiet for a season, but that season is now ending. You know what God has done in your life, and you will no longer keep silent about it. You know you are a sinner saved by grace, just like everybody else on the planet who has chosen to follow Jesus. So if you can offer hope and light, love and grace to someone else going through the same kinds of storms and shipwrecks you've endured, praise God!

Your suffering is not for nothing. Even though others may have intended to silence you, arrest you, hurt you, bankrupt you, divorce you, betray you, abuse you, fire you, or abandon you, God turned it around and saved you! Even though the Enemy tried to use your wounds to sideline you, you are back in the game. Your scars from the shipwreck are now God's trophies of grace.

Still struggling to see how God can use you? Consider another person caught in undesirable weather on open water and forced to face his fears: Jesus's disciple Peter. Next to Paul, Peter may be the disciple that intrigues me the most, primarily because he's up one minute and down the next—sometimes literally!

> Shortly before dawn Jesus went out to them, walking on the lake. When the disciples saw him walking on the lake, they were terrified. "It's a ghost," they said, and cried out in fear.
>
> But Jesus immediately said to them: "Take courage! It is I. Don't be afraid."
>
> "Lord, if it's you," Peter replied, "tell me to come to you on the water."
>
> "Come," he said.

Then Peter got down out of the boat, walked on the water and came toward Jesus. But when he saw the wind, he was afraid and, beginning to sink, cried out, "Lord, save me!"

Immediately Jesus reached out his hand and caught him. "You of little faith," he said, "why did you doubt?" (Matthew 14:25–31)

I love the contrast here between what the disciples perceived and what was true. At first they thought they saw a ghost coming toward their boat—what else could it be, right? They didn't know anyone who could walk on water, and apparently Jesus had not demonstrated his lake-walking technique prior to this encounter. Then Peter, just like Gideon and all of us, asked for proof: "If it's really you, God, let me do the impossible!" This is what we all say at some point as we struggle to get out of the boat of our fear and shame.

> ## Step by step we're doing what we could never imagine or accomplish on our own.

"Come," the Lord tells us, so we step out of the boat and put our feet on the water. Step by step we're doing what we could never imagine or accomplish on our own. We're doing something so amazing, so miraculous, so unheard of that it surprises us along with the rest of the world. But then we have a moment, like Peter, when we take our eyes off God and instead focus on our human perspective, on the weather, on our inadequacy. We start to sink, allowing doubt and fear and shame over our past to become quicksand and swallow our progress, but not before God reaches out and grabs us, rescuing us from storms of our own making.

It's significant to me that Peter later denied even knowing Jesus after spending the night in Gethsemane with Christ and some of the other disciples. After Jesus was arrested, Peter sank into fear and claimed he'd never met Jesus. And he told this lie not just once but *three* times (see Luke 22:54–62). Peter's denial of Jesus was far from the end of his story, however. Jesus knew what Peter could become. Earlier he had said, "I tell you, you are Peter, and on this rock I will build my church, and the gates of hell shall not prevail against it" (Matthew 16:18, ESV). Pretty amazing words if you consider that Christ was talking to the same guy who'd sunk in the water and would deny knowing Jesus during one of the darkest hours of Jesus's life on earth. This is what our God can do. He transformed Peter's doubts and fears into a bedrock of faith and trust—just the kind of foundation needed for Christ's church.

God wants to build on the foundation of our faith as well. We have nothing to fear, and the Enemy cannot harm us with his venomous accusations. Shame over who we used to be or what we've done in the past cannot bind us any longer. "Anyone who belongs to Christ has become a new person. The old life is gone; a new life has begun!" (2 Corinthians 5:17, NLT).

EVERYTHING YOU NEED

When we've made it through storms and reached the shore, when we've survived shipwrecks and snakebites, when we're willing to let God work through the parts of our lives that the Enemy attacked, then we're going to experience God's favor. After Paul healed all the sick people on the island of Malta, God favored him by prompting the people there to furnish him with everything he needed to continue on his journey to Rome.

When we're obedient to God and willing for him to win others through our wounds, he will sustain us and equip us for what's ahead. We're promised, "God is able to bless you abundantly, so that in all things at all times, having all that you need, you will abound in every good work" (2 Corinthians 9:8). Our Father, the Creator of the heavens and the earth and everything that exists, has unlimited resources. We will receive exactly what we need when we need it. "My God will meet all your needs according to the riches of his glory in Christ Jesus" (Philippians 4:19).

Nonetheless, we may still have "Gotcha!" moments when we're caught off guard and briefly waver. Whenever we step out in faith and risk being used by God, at some point we will likely wonder—and possibly even worry—about how we will continue on our journeys. We'll be walking on water when suddenly we panic and feel certain we're about to sink and drown. While we've seen God come through time after time, saving us and providing for us and blessing us with all we've needed, we will likely be tempted by the Enemy to doubt God's goodness and power going forward. "Sure, God got you this far—barely! After that storm almost wiped you out and the ship crashed! After that snake scared you half to death! After all that, do you really think he cares what happens to you? He's never going to get you to Rome, so you might as well give up now." Is that what Satan might have whispered to Paul?

In those moments you must be strong and remember that the devil gives you problems, but God gives you purpose! What God has placed in you is greater than what the devil has placed in front of you. Today is the day you will stand up and occupy the very area hell has fought to keep you out of.

Shipwreck survivors don't just swim in God's favor—*they walk on water*!

SHAKE FREE . . . FROM SHAME

Reflect on the following questions as you consider how God wants to continue transforming your struggles with his strength. Ask his Spirit to guide you as you think about your answers and how God might be speaking to your heart at this time.

1. How have you seen God work through your weaknesses in the past? How have you been able to bless others because of what you've endured and triumphed over?

2. What areas of your life or incidents in your past continue to ignite shame? Has this sense of shame prevented you from being obedient to God and fulfilling the calling he's placed on your life?

3. What other ways besides shame have you seen the Enemy try to attack you and derail your testimony and ministry? How have you handled these attacks? What promises of God from his Word do you need to keep before you to guard your heart against such assaults? Choose one verse—one of your favorites or one mentioned in this chapter—and write it out below, claiming it as a shield against the venom of the Enemy.

_____

Lord, I marvel at all you've done for me and through me up to this point in my life. I never could have survived all the storms and shipwrecks I've encountered without your protection and provision each and every day. Thank you for using them to make me stronger and to deepen my faith in you. Forgive me for the times when I still give in to temptation and doubt you, fearing I'll sink in the rough waters around me rather than walk on them, just as Peter did that day with Jesus. Your grace is the remedy for shame, and the Enemy's accusations have no power over me. You have already defeated him, and death has no sting. Thank you for loving me and working through me to display your glory and shine your light of love into the darkness of the world around me. Amen.

13

If You Can Make It to Malta, You Can Make It to Rome

People don't take trips—trips take people.

—John Steinbeck,
Travels with Charley in Search of America

've never been to Malta, but I've visited Pittsburgh a few times. While it may sound strange, the two places have more in common than you might think. I'm certainly not comparing myself to Paul, but just as his layover in Malta prepared him for continuing his journey to Rome, my visits to Pittsburgh back when I was a youth pastor equipped me for where God was taking me. Let me explain.

Some people believe that youth pastors have it easy. They think that youth ministry is often the training ground for new pastors because it allows them to ramp up to real ministry later in their lives. Casual observers assume that rather than contributing to the "serious" work of the church, which the senior pastor and other team members do, youth pastors just hang out with kids and have fun. They see them meet kids after school and on weekends, play games, and go to concerts, amusement parks, and ball games. Throw in a prayer or Bible story now and then, and how hard can it be?

The reality—ask anyone who has ever ministered to youth—is just the opposite. Youth ministry can often be the hardest area in which to communicate the truth of the gospel and serve the needs of hurting people. Tweens and teens, particularly in our tech-driven world of social media, are making the difficult, often painful transition from childhood to adulthood. They're longing for adult independence—and facing all the temptations that come with it—while struggling with leaving behind the innocence and security of being a kid.

They're facing the storms of life for the first time.

And they're looking for a lifeline.

FIELD TRIP OF FAITH

Any pastor with a burden for the precious lives of young people quickly learns that you can't give pat answers or fake your faith. These searching, hurting, hungry-for-truth hearts simply won't have it. Used to putting up facades and defenses of their own, teens can smell a phony a mile away. If they sense you're not sincere in your concern for them or don't really believe what you're preaching, they're out the door faster than you can say *amen*.

And all those crazy events, seasonal activities, and fun field trips? Youth pastors know that those situations often provide opportunities for kids to let their guards down and open up about their hopes and fears, doubts and questions. Removed from the watching eyes of peers in their schools and neighborhoods and the expectations of parents, young people often reveal their true selves and their aching need for Jesus.

That kind of transparency was certainly my experience on the trips our church youth group would make from Allentown, where most of us lived, to the Steel City for a ball game or concert. We would load up in a couple of church vans and make the road trip, roughly a five-hour drive each way, as tolerable as possible. If we spent the night, either at a sister church or in a hotel, there was even more time together to nonchalantly talk about what mattered most to them.

I was put on the spot more than a few times during these trips. I remember one young lady in particular. Outgoing and popular at school, she let her mask slip while away on these youth group excursions, revealing a sincere desire to know the truth about God, life, and relationships. When I talked with her and a few others, she would never let me off the hook, often following up my answers and explanations with an honest refrain of "But why?"

She reminded me of the way preschoolers, eager to discover and understand the world, sometimes question parents and teachers about everything. Only this young lady didn't want to know what giraffes eat or how yogurt is made, as a little kid might. She wanted to know whether God really cared about her parents' divorce, whether she should sleep with her boyfriend, or where she should go to college. She longed to understand why Jesus had to die on the cross and why his heavenly Father would make such an unimaginable sacrifice.

Through honest conversations with her and dozens of other earnest young men and women, I received an education that can't be taught in any ministry class or Bible college. I learned how to hold God's Word close, not to prove a point or defend my position but simply to support the basis for my own faith. I faced numerous crisis moments with these kids, from the minor and relatively benign (braces, bad haircuts, breakups) to the major and deeply troubling (suicide attempts, drug addiction, domestic abuse).

My experiences as a youth leader not only made me a better pastor; they made me a better man. Those discussions, prayers, private moments, and public milestones forced me to depend on God and rely on his guidance on a daily, sometimes hourly, basis. I discovered more about how God made me and the calling he had on my life. My faith was strengthened and my character was refined.

I could never do what I'm doing now without having gone to Pittsburgh!

PATIENCE FOR PROMISES

If you look at the lives of the faithful people in Scripture, many of them went through some kind of Malta of their own—some kind of season, storm, or shipwreck that prepared them for reaching their destinations and fulfilling their divine purposes. Such seasons of preparation usually required them to be patient as well—and then be patient some more!

The people of Israel experienced this process as they called out to God to deliver them from slavery in Egypt. They had ended up there because a terrible famine sent them scrambling south for food, most notably when Joseph's brothers showed up begging for grain and received the shock of their lives. Not only was their baby brother still alive after all those years, but he was now in charge of the country, directly under Pharaoh! Even more amazing, Joseph was willing to forgive them for nearly killing him before selling him as a slave. As he explained to them, "You intended to harm me, but God intended it for good to accomplish what is now being done, the saving of many lives" (Genesis 50:20).

Fast-forward four hundred years and those many lives that were saved soon outnumbered the native Egyptians, who feared that their Hebrew visitors would take over and claim Egypt as their own. As the Israelites' numbers multiplied with each new generation, so did their complaints before God. They would have remembered and repeated the stories of their ancestors, especially the ones about Abraham and the promises God made to him. As the years dragged on and their conditions grew worse, the Hebrew people struggled to believe that God would honor those promises.

We often react the same way. When we arrive in Malta instead of Rome, when God doesn't act on our timetable, we're tempted to dismiss his promises or assume he's forgotten us. That's simply not true!

Just as Abraham was faithful, we must cling to God's promises, particularly when we're temporarily stranded on the way to our divine destinations. We're told, "Abraham never wavered in believing God's promise. In fact, his faith grew stronger, and in this he brought glory to God. He was fully convinced that God is able to do whatever he promises" (Romans 4:20–21, NLT).

Whether you're in Malta, Pittsburgh, or somewhere else, God has not forgotten you. He is there with you, just as he promised, preparing you for the next leg of your journey. When you find yourself growing impatient and wondering whether you've missed the boat, when you wonder whether life has passed you by and the best years are behind you, then stop and remember the purpose God has for you. If he's placed a calling on your life and prepared you for his purposes, he will get you to Rome one way or another!

JETLAG JITTERS

During life's layovers, we simply have to be patient and wait on God's timing, reminding ourselves that he is never far from us:

> From one man he made all the nations, that they should inhabit the
> whole earth; and he marked out their appointed times in history and
> the boundaries of their lands. God did this so that they would seek him
> and perhaps reach out for him and find him, though he is not far from
> any one of us. (Acts 17:26–27)

Waiting is not always easy, though, as you stroll the shores of your temporary Malta, pacing back and forth. Even after God has protected you and demonstrated his miraculous power to get you this far, your memories tend to be as selective as those of the Israelites after leaving Egypt. They had witnessed God bring unbelievable plagues to their captors, even as he protected them and split the Red Sea to ensure their escape.

But then their journey didn't go as expected. Instead of trotting across the desert to beautiful new homes in Milk-and-Honey Meadows, they wandered across the dunes, dirty and tired and hungry—for years and then more years! Eventually, they even regretted leaving Egypt and whined that it would be better to have died or be back in slavery than to follow God to the Promised Land:

In the desert the whole community grumbled against Moses
and Aaron. The Israelites said to them, "If only we had died by
the LORD's hand in Egypt! There we sat around pots of meat
and ate all the food we wanted, but you have brought us out
into this desert to starve this entire assembly to death." (Exodus
16:2–3)

Just as we often panic when our pleasure cruise becomes the *Titanic,* the
Israelites didn't handle their disappointment very well. They wished they had
been killed back in Egypt rather than having to suffer while trudging through
the desert toward the place God had for them. To put it simply, they lost sight
of their purpose and God's promises. They suffered from extended travel fatigue, or what I call the jetlag jitters. If you've ever been on a long trip that goes
beyond days into weeks, particularly if it involves traveling through cultures
different from your own, you know what I'm talking about.

Travel fatigue causes hard-core vegans to run to Burger King and trans-
forms even the most mature, mild-mannered saints into screaming preschoolers. You don't know whether it's morning, noon, or night—or even which time
zone you're in. Your body aches, and all you want to do is close your eyes and
sleep, but even when you try, a weary restlessness gnaws at your mind and body.
If you're traveling with small children, your fatigue becomes compounded by
theirs. It's not so much "Are we there yet?" as it is a sense of "Will we *ever* be
there? Because I'm not sure I'm going to make it!"

ALMOST THERE

But if you can make it to Malta, you can make it to Rome. If you can make it
out of Egypt, you can make it to the Promised Land. Remember, God has not
brought you this far to let you wither and die short of your destination. He has

done the impossible to get you to where you are now, and he will continue to do whatever it takes to help you reach the place you need to be.

While the Israelites wandered and waited in the desert, God provided for them time and time again. He gave them bread from heaven, called manna, along with quail and dew each morning for hydration (see Exodus 16:1–18). He also continued to direct them: "By day the LORD went ahead of them in a pillar of cloud to guide them on their way and by night in a pillar of fire to give them light, so that they could travel by day or night" (13:21). It wasn't what they expected or delivered the way they expected, but nonetheless God took care of them and provided for all their needs. Like a patient, loving parent attending a fussy child on a long trip, God endured their grumbling and complaining and gave them what they needed each step of the way. He still does the same for each of us.

Our impatience makes us feel as though our time in Malta will never end. We feel stuck—so close to our destinations and yet so far away. Strangely enough, sometimes it feels even harder to trust God when you know you're so close to where he's taking you. You're almost there but not quite. Rome is within sight, but you still have a few miles to go. You're excited but weary, hopeful but cautious.

Because we'd rather speed up the process and minimize our suffering and discomfort, it's tough to glimpse Rome but not actually be there yet. These are the times when you see a positive change in your spouse's attitude and can envision God healing your marriage. These are the moments when you begin to gain control of your finances and dig slowly out of debt; some bills are paid, but there's still progress to be made. These are the seasons when your body finally turns a corner and you know you're feeling better, even though weeks of physical therapy remain.

During these times we must remember that we're right where God wants us. As much as we'd like to pick up the pace and move ahead, we just have to take a deep breath and keep going, one step after another, hour after hour, one day to the next. And while we're working to align our expectations with God's sense of timing, we must not overlook the many blessings we have in the present moment and the ways we can serve others right where we are.

Too often we're so impatient to get to Rome and do the "really important work" God has called us to do that we neglect the small acts of kindness and habits of service that got us on the journey in the first place. We're told, "Whoever can be trusted with very little can also be trusted with much" (Luke 16:10), and this applies whether we're waiting in Malta or arriving in Rome.

We mustn't forget the spiritual practices and daily disciplines that keep us connected to God. Mother Teresa said, "Be faithful in small things because it is in them that your strength lies." Don't stop doing what you know you should do just because you're getting close to your breakthrough!

Temporary Layovers

Paul was not supposed to land in Malta; he was supposed to land in Rome. Sometimes life will take us to places that are temporary as we head toward our ultimate destinations, but even in those places the favor of God will be present. During our layovers, we will be given resources for the next chapter of our stories, the next leg of our journeys. We will be equipped for what we're about to encounter.

Even after Paul sailed from Malta and arrived on the Italian mainland, it still took him a while to get to Rome. Notice all the places mentioned from the time he left Malta until he actually set foot in Rome:

> After three months we put out to sea in a ship that had wintered in the island—it was an Alexandrian ship with the figurehead of the twin gods Castor and Pollux. We put in at Syracuse and stayed there three days. From there we set sail and arrived at Rhegium. The next day the south

wind came up, and on the following day we reached Puteoli. There we found some brothers and sisters who invited us to spend a week with them. And so we came to Rome. The brothers and sisters there had heard that we were coming, and they traveled as far as the Forum of Appius and the Three Taverns to meet us. At the sight of these people Paul thanked God and was encouraged. (Acts 28:11–15)

After three months in Malta, Paul and his shipmates finally sailed to Syracuse, a major port city on the southeast coast of Sicily. A sizable island that's now part of Italy, Sicily looks like the football being kicked by the long boot of the Italian peninsula. From Syracuse, they sailed north to Rhegium, now known as Reggio Calabria, the city situated right on the toe of the boot. According to the ancient writer Aeschylus, this city's name comes from the Greek word meaning "to split" or "to rend," a reference to the break between the mainland and Sicily.*

From Rhegium, Paul's ship ventured northwest along the coast of Italy until anchoring in Puteoli, a beautiful harbor and major shipping area that's now part of the city of Naples. And there Paul must have felt that joy of arrival we've all experienced before—that moment when we first set foot in a new destination, welcomed by friendly, familiar faces.

These brothers and sisters were other believers who had received word that Paul was on his way and had finally arrived. Still under the supervision of Julius, the kindly disposed centurion from the Roman Imperial Regiment (see 27:1), Paul was allowed to stay and relax with this welcoming party for a full week before continuing to Rome by foot. If you've ever traveled cross-country or overseas, you know how wonderful it feels to have a loved one waiting to welcome you.

Apparently these weren't Paul's only fans in Italy, because once he set out

---

* "Rhegium," BiblePlaces.com, www.bibleplaces.com/rhegium.

for Rome, a distance of roughly 150 miles, he was met by two other landing parties. One intercepted Paul near the Forum of Appius, about forty miles south of Rome, and another at Three Taverns, approximately thirty miles south of the Italian capital. "At the sight of these people Paul thanked God and was encouraged" (28:15). After all he'd been through—and fully aware of what he was to face in Rome—Paul needed this emotional and spiritual support just as much as he needed food, water, and shelter after landing in Malta.

The beauty and timing of God's provision never ceases to amaze me. I can't tell you how many times I've been running on fumes—physically, mentally, and emotionally depleted—when suddenly God brought gracious people of faith across my path. Some invited me into their home for a meal or a night's rest before I delivered God's message the next day. Others hosted me for days on end, joyfully attending to my every need while I participated in a ministry conference or church event. Some simply came up to me in a parking lot, an airport terminal, or a hotel lobby and asked whether they could pray for me.

> ## The beauty and timing of God's provision never ceases to amaze.

Never forget that if God can meet your physical and material needs, he can surely meet your spiritual and emotional needs. Don't be surprised as you're arriving in Rome to be greeted by brothers and sisters eager to welcome you and help you. And don't be too proud to accept their hospitality and rest in their kindness. God uses us to support one another. Always welcome other Christians with the affection and encouragement that's unique to the family of God. You never know where someone else might be going—or whether their Rome is your neighborhood!

Once you enter Rome, you can look back and see how far you've come. Then you can often understand why God chose the route he used to get you there. You can finally see that your unscheduled layover in Malta (or in Pittsburgh!) was more than necessary for what you're about to face.

So remain patient, my friend, as you get closer and closer to your divine destination. If you can make it to Malta, you can assuredly make it to Rome.

You're almost there!

SHAKE FREE . . . FROM IMPATIENCE

Use the following questions to think about how far you've come on your journey of faith—all the highs and lows, the storms you've survived, and the new shores you're still exploring. As you reflect on how God has brought you to where you are right now, relax and trust his perfect sense of timing for where you're going next.

1. What are some of the most severe storms you've survived in your life? How did God protect and sustain you through each one? What have you learned about yourself through these difficult times? What have you learned about God?

2. How close to Rome are you right now in your life's journey? In other words, how close are you to being exactly where God wants you to serve him and have the greatest impact? In what ways do you find yourself struggling to be patient as you get closer to your Rome?

3. When have you experienced a place of resting, regrouping, and recovering as Paul found in Malta? How did your time there prepare you for where God wanted to take you next? How did your time there prepare you for where you are right now?

4. When was the last time another believer encouraged you in your faith? How did it help you? When was the last time you encouraged someone else? Is there someone you need to call, text, or meet with simply to listen to each other and pray together?

Jesus, you know all the ups and downs of my life, all the mountaintop experiences as well as those times when I've walked through the valley of the shadow. Thank you for remaining close by my side every step of the way and carrying me when I didn't think I could keep going. I feel so close to a breakthrough now, and I know my Rome is right around the corner! Give me the patience I need today, Lord, and help me trust you and wait on your timing instead of rushing ahead. Continue to use my present location to prepare me for what's next, and give me eyes to see how I can love and serve those around me, just as those brothers and sisters in Italy encouraged Paul. Help me wait calmly in Malta until it's time to go to Rome. Amen.

14

In Rome at Last!

Here was Rome indeed at last; and such
a Rome as no one can imagine in its full
and awful grandeur!

—Charles Dickens, *Pictures from Italy*

When I was fourteen, I began my own voyage to Rome. It was a spiritual journey, not literal, although my travels would indeed take me through the ancient Italian capital and allow me to stand where Paul himself might have stood. My divinely appointed route has taken me around the world, from Rome to Rio, from Sacramento to Sydney, from Waco to Washington. Whenever I pause to look back at my life and take in the view, I can't help but marvel at how God has brought me to where I am today.

As you know by now, I was a quiet nerd in school, more interested in playing Nintendo and listening to Van Halen than being the center of attention. The last thing I could ever have imagined—and even then only in a nightmare—would be speaking in front of thousands of people. Totally unimaginable was being a few feet away from the president of the United States as I offered a prayer at his inauguration before millions of people watching live around the world. How has all this come about?

One night in 1983, God's Spirit began stirring my heart. It had been a regular school day, and as usual I'd finished my homework and enjoyed dinner with my family. Then before bedtime I turned on the TV in our family room and began flipping channels, likely hoping to find an old episode of *Star Trek* or sneak in a music video on MTV. Instead, I paused on a channel featuring a well-known televangelist delivering a passionate sermon to a huge crowd in a packed auditorium.

Samuel, one day that will be you preaching in front of so many people. You're going to do that someday! I heard that message in my heart and knew it was true. I didn't know where the words came from or even exactly what they meant, but I knew this message provided a glimpse into the future God had for me.

Soon the sermon ended and I flipped channels again, this time landing on a PBS special on the life of Dr. Martin Luther King Jr. I was well aware of the famous civil rights leader's role in overturning segregation, but as I watched clips of him preaching and delivering his brilliant, timeless speeches, once again I felt something stir inside. *That's what you will be doing,* the voice within whispered. *You were made to speak and lead and champion God's love to people everywhere. That will be you someday!*

As a shy kid with little interest in public speaking or pastoral vocations, I wasn't sure what to make of my television epiphany that night. My parents were not preachers or ministers. They were Christians and raised me in a warm, loving environment, but no one expected me to pursue full-time ministry. But I never forgot what I felt inside that night or the calling God placed within me to follow him to my Rome.

PROPHETIC AND PRACTICAL

As I grew into young adulthood, I continued to follow God and honor the calling he had placed on my life. I, the shy computer geek, had been transformed into a young man passionate about the gospel of Jesus Christ, the love of God, and the power of his Spirit within me. I wanted to minister and serve not only horizontally—person-to-person here on earth—but also vertically as I advanced God's kingdom. I wanted to fight the good fight I read about in the Bible (see 2 Timothy 4:7) so that all people could experience the abundant life Jesus told us he came to bring (see John 10:10).

Doors began to open for me to speak and lead within my church, denomination, and community. In some ways the invitations and opportunities happened so easily, but I know they were supernaturally arranged. Other pastors would ask me to preach in their churches or speak at their conferences. Afterward, they always encouraged me. "We really see something in you," they would tell me. "God has big plans for you!"

Their encouragement has often fueled my journey amid the storms and shipwrecks of my life. And I quickly learned that my desire to combine horizontal and vertical ministries, my passion for fusing the evangelism of Billy Graham with the social justice and activism of Dr. King, was not always warmly received. Some people have considered me too political. Others have criticized me for taking various stands against injustice and prejudice.

You see, I don't like the way Christianity often gets defined in our society today. Over the past four or five decades, the perception of Christians, particularly evangelicals, has been characterized by what others believe—or assume—we're *against*. So many people want to view followers of Jesus as extremists who are summed up by one word: *anti*. Anti-liberal, anti-abortion, anti-gay, anti-whatever.

That's not what Jesus came to teach us. The Christian faith is defined more accurately by what it's for than anything others think we're against. We are pro-compassion, pro-charity, pro-faith, pro-service, pro-hope, pro-healing—on and on! The love of God and the power of his Spirit in our lives are transformative. Christianity reinvigorates and revitalizes rather than obstructs and oppresses.

Historically, in my humble opinion, white evangelicals in our country focused too narrowly on the vertical aspects of our faith. African American Christians, on the other hand, focused horizontally—in large part because they had to. Dr. King and many other leaders ushered in an emphasis on attaining social justice, overcoming racism and discrimination, and improving impoverished lives. My passion, going back all the way to that night when I was fourteen, is to merge the two.

We're not the only ones bridging the two, of course, but I believe that Hispanic Christians in the US, the fastest-growing demographic of Christians, have an anointed opportunity to redefine Christianity in a way that balances the vertical and horizontal planes of our faith. We can combine sanctification with service, conviction with compassion, the character of God with the habits of Christ, holiness with humility—the themes of John 3:13 and Matthew 25. We can be both prophetic and practical, in the world but not of the world, present in the moment and prepared for eternity.

My passion and dedication for expanding God's kingdom, the most perfect blend of all these aspects of our faith, now continues as I minister from the platform he has given me. God has brought me to my own personal Rome for his purposes, and I continue to humbly serve where he leads, following the example of strength and gentleness modeled by Jesus. Whether with presidents or the impoverished, with celebrities or shy teens who remind me of myself, I serve as God's ambassador to those around me. And, just like Paul, I continue to experience the favor of the Lord in the most unexpected ways.

ROMAN HOLIDAY

When Paul arrived in Rome, he must have felt a mixture of relief and excitement. He probably thanked God for getting him there through so many obstacles and great adversity. But Paul may have also wondered what he was in for now that he was there.

The dynamic Italian capital into which he strolled in AD 60 served as home to about a million people, by far the largest city in the world at that time. As the heart of the vast Roman Empire, the city displayed the extremes of human existence, showcasing the wealth and power of the Roman elite as well as the poverty and struggle of the many slaves brought there from various lands the empire had conquered.

City walls formed a thirteen-mile perimeter around Rome. Massive monuments and construction projects, along with numerous temples to various Roman deities, clustered next to multistory apartment buildings housing thousands of poor citizens and slaves. Situated strategically along the Tiber River, the city was divided into more than a dozen districts, including the famous Circus Maximus and the Forum Romanum.

The forum pulsed as the heartbeat of Rome's political, social, economic, and religious life and included the Senate, the Mamertime prison, a vast marketplace, and various shrines to past caesars as well as to Nero, the emperor at that time. Only a few miles away, in the valley between the Aventine and Palatine Hills, where the palaces of the caesars loomed, the Circus Maximus was a large open-air stadium where chariot races (think *Ben-Hur* and *Spartacus*), other sporting events, and vendors attracted crowds regularly. One of the best-known historic sites in Rome, the Colosseum, would not be built for another twenty years after Paul's arrival.[*]

Amid the hustle and bustle of the thriving Roman capital, Paul was not there as a tourist or even an evangelist but as a prisoner. Even so, he still experienced the favor of God, in ways large and small:

When we got to Rome, Paul was allowed to live by himself, with a soldier to guard him.

Three days later he called together the local Jewish leaders. When

---

[*] Clinton E. Arnold, "Acts," in *Zondervan Illustrated Bible Backgrounds Commentary*, ed. Clinton E. Arnold, vol. 2, *John, Acts* (Grand Rapids, MI: Zondervan, 2002), 482.

they had assembled, Paul said to them: "My brothers, although I have done nothing against our people or against the customs of our ancestors, I was arrested in Jerusalem and handed over to the Romans. They examined me and wanted to release me, because I was not guilty of any crime deserving death. The Jews objected, so I was compelled to make an appeal to Caesar. I certainly did not intend to bring any charge against my own people. For this reason I have asked to see you and talk with you. It is because of the hope of Israel that I am bound with this chain."

They replied, "We have not received any letters from Judea concerning you, and none of our people who have come from there has reported or said anything bad about you. But we want to hear what your views are, for we know that people everywhere are talking against this sect."

They arranged to meet Paul on a certain day, and came in even larger numbers to the place where he was staying. He witnessed to them from morning till evening, explaining about the kingdom of God, and from the Law of Moses and from the Prophets he tried to persuade them about Jesus. (Acts 28:16–23)

Paul was finally accomplishing in Rome what God had intended for him all along, but not without new challenges.

RUMOR HAS IT

After you achieve your goal or realize your dream, you may be disoriented at first. You know you're right where God wants you, but you will likely still encounter new obstacles and old struggles. In other words, just because you've arrived in Rome, life may not seem easier. When God elevates you to a new position of authority or creates a platform of privilege for you, it can be stressful. The pressure is often greater. The people are often more powerful. The problems are often bigger.

But so is your favor with God!

Paul experienced this firsthand after arriving in Rome. For starters, he was allowed to live by himself in a small apartment, not in a prison cell. You don't have to be an expert historian to know this was not the norm! Although a Roman soldier continued to guard him, Paul enjoyed the freedom of movement that would allow him to interact with numerous other people, including the Jewish religious leaders, the first ones Paul invited over for a visit to his new crib.

Once these leaders gathered, Paul explained how he came to stand before them. Being as diplomatic as possible, he basically said, "Although I've done nothing to hurt anyone or damage the reputation of the Jewish people, they seem to have a problem with me. I was arrested, and the Roman officials wanted to release me, but the Jewish leaders kept squawking. So I asked to go before Caesar to clear things up once and for all. I'm in these chains as a prisoner in hopes of winning over my own people!"

In return, the Jewish officials revealed, "Hey, we're not sure what you're talking about, Paul. We've received no paperwork and haven't heard anything bad about you. But since you're here, we'd love to know what you have to say about all this business with Jesus and his followers."

Can you believe it? Paul's court documents got lost in the mail!

When you finally arrive in the Rome where God wants you, don't be surprised to experience his favor. Yes, there will still be challenges, frustrations, and disappointments. But after God has brought you through storms, shipwrecks, and snakebites, don't you think he will continue to open a way for you?

When you're right where God wants you, he will free you from the chains of culture, society, government, and any other obstacle impeding you from doing his work. In God's Word we read, "LORD, the God of our ancestors, are you not the God who is in heaven? You rule over all the kingdoms of the nations. Power and might are in your hand, and no one can withstand you" (2 Chronicles 20:6).

Did you get that? *No one can withstand the power of God!* Not the Jewish leaders persecuting Paul nor the Roman soldiers required to guard him and escort him to Rome. Not the debt collector calling to harass you night and day. Not the ex-spouse battling over the well-being of your children. Not the neighbor gossiping about you behind your back. Not the boss who continually takes credit for your work. Not the science-reliant doctor with the grim diagnosis.

No one!

FOR ALL PEOPLE

Since they hadn't received any documents, the Jewish leaders didn't have any reason or legal basis for holding Paul. Nonetheless, they were curious and eager to listen to what he had to say. He apparently impressed them as someone who was respectable, intelligent, and well spoken—not a crazy man babbling about someone back in Jerusalem who supposedly had returned from the dead.

Paul's opponents likely didn't have anything against him personally; they were opposed to followers of Jesus in general. Many of them perceived Jesus as a heretic and cult leader, just as Paul once had prior to meeting the Lord on the road to Damascus. Even after Jesus was arrested, crucified, and buried, his followers continued to teach his ways, which opposed strict Jewish customs according to the law of Moses. To put it simply, many Jewish leaders could not grasp—and apparently weren't willing to try—the concept of grace, the essence of the gospel of Jesus Christ.

Still, Paul's heart remained burdened for these very people. He had been one of them—remember, it takes one to know one!—and he knew that God had called him to Rome to preach the gospel. Many scholars believe there were about fifty thousand Jews living in Rome at the time of Paul's visit.* Paul wanted them to hear firsthand—not from the rumor mill back home—who Jesus really is and what grace is all about. And as Paul made clear to his esteemed guests, the good news is not only for Jews—it's for all people.

Never one to mince words, Paul proceeded boldly and told these Jewish leaders in Rome the truth:

> Some were convinced by what he said, but others would not believe. They disagreed among themselves and began to leave after Paul had made this final statement: "The Holy Spirit spoke the truth to your ancestors when he said through Isaiah the prophet:
>
>> "'Go to this people and say,
>> "You will be ever hearing but never understanding;
>>> you will be ever seeing but never perceiving."
>> For this people's heart has become calloused;
>>> they hardly hear with their ears,
>>> and they have closed their eyes.
>> Otherwise they might see with their eyes,
>>> hear with their ears,
>>> understand with their hearts
>> and turn, and I would heal them.'
>
> "Therefore I want you to know that God's salvation has been sent to the Gentiles, and they will listen!" (Acts 28:24–28)

---

* Albert Barnes, "Paul in Rome," *Scenes and Incidents in the Life of the Apostle Paul*, Bible Study Tools, www .biblestudytools.com/classics/barnes-scenes-in-life/paul-in-rome/.

Paul quoted from Isaiah (see 6:9–10) not only because the passage was familiar to his audience but also because the ancient prophet's message so perfectly addressed their situation. Throughout the history of Israel and across the pages of the Old Testament, God pursued his chosen people despite their on-again, off-again response to him. In spite of all God did for them—rescuing them from slavery in Egypt, providing for them in the desert, and leading them to the Promised Land, just to name a few biggies—the Jewish people chose not to remain faithful. They allowed their hearts to wander, and their idolatry hardened them to the love of God.

In his omniscience, God knew what would happen when he sent his only Son to earth as the long-promised Messiah. Jesus's arrival on the scene turned the Jewish world upside down. No longer must they depend on a merit system of obeying laws as they worked toward a holiness they could never achieve. No longer must they sacrifice animals for temporary forgiveness before God. No longer did their sin separate them from God's love.

We get so hung up on our differences.

With his sacrificial death on the cross, resurrection to life, and gift of the Holy Spirit, Jesus opened a portal between heaven and earth. Christ merged the vertical and horizontal dimensions of ministry, saving people from their sins while serving them and meeting their needs. He set a new standard for obeying God and provided a new model of relating to the Father based on personal relationship—not external behavior, worldly achievement, or feelings of shame or regret.

This is what excites me about my job! This is why I'm so thrilled to be in the Rome that God has brought me to serve in. I'm privileged to serve others in the name of Jesus and called to address all their needs—physical, emotional, and spiritual—just as Christ himself did. And this calling is not just for me or people in full-time vocational ministry. God calls each of us to minister where we are and serve those around us. Paul reminds us, "There is neither Jew nor Gentile, neither slave nor free, nor is there male and female, for you are all one in Christ Jesus" (Galatians 3:28).

It doesn't matter who you are, where you come from, or what you've done or haven't done. It doesn't matter whether you dropped out of high school or earned a PhD, whether you're ending a relationship or starting a new ministry, whether you're black or white, brown or yellow, Democrat or Republican, male or female, rich or poor, young or old. None of that matters before God!

We get so hung up on our differences and allow those differences to breed fear, anger, bitterness, prejudice, and violence in our hearts. We get swept up in power struggles and factions, in politics and divisions, but the God who made us, in whose image every single human being is created, unites us all! He knows our hearts and wants to fill the holes inside our lives that only Jesus can fill. He knows that our humanity unites us much more than any individual differences divide us.

This is the noble calling you have today wherever God has placed you:

- to live in the freedom and love of Jesus Christ
- to fulfill the unique purpose God has given you
- to share with everyone around you what you know and have experienced

WITH ALL BOLDNESS

Once Paul arrived in Rome, he was there for a while and definitely made the most of it:

For two whole years Paul stayed there in his own rented house and welcomed all who came to see him. He proclaimed the kingdom of God and taught about the Lord Jesus Christ—with all boldness and without hindrance! (Acts 28:30–31)

Many New Testament scholars debate where Paul went—or whether he even left Rome—after the two years mentioned here. Regardless of what he did afterward, it's clear he had an enormous impact during those two years. It's striking to me that Paul managed to proclaim the gospel and share about Jesus Christ "with all boldness and without hindrance" (verse 31). You'll recall that it was Paul's boldness that got him in trouble back in Jerusalem in the first place. His arrest there set in motion his journey to Rome. But again, perceptions are not reality. What appeared to be Paul's trip to Rome as a prisoner to face the Roman courts became a miraculous adventure of God's provision and protection culminating in Paul's doing what God had brought him to Rome to do: proclaim the good news of grace through Jesus!

The fact that Paul was able to preach so freely without hindrance is amazing. There in the capital of the mighty Roman Empire—with plenty of soldiers, guards, senators, and noblemen likely crossing paths with him each day—the bold apostle was never stopped, accosted, heckled, or arrested. We're not told specifically, but I have to believe that many people from all walks of life came to know the Lord because they heard Paul preach in Rome during those two incredible years.

Once you've reached your Rome, you can live out your purpose with the same boldness Paul displayed. When you arrive where you know God wants you, there's no time for being shy about how and why God got you there. Even if other people or circumstances hinder you, don't be discouraged from doing what you were born to do.

Doubt is the destroyer of destiny! So make the most of your arrival and learn all that God has for you in Rome. Bask in his favor and the deep soul fulfillment that comes from living a purpose-driven, passion-fueled life. If you're not there yet, keep going and remember the faithful patience and perseverance of Paul. Once God called him to Rome, he didn't let anyone or anything keep him from his divine appointment with destiny.

Doubt is the destroyer of destiny!

As you continue to step out in faith and follow God's path for your life, you, too, have an appointment with destiny.

God's favor is upon you, and no storm can wash it away.

God's favor is upon you, and no shipwreck can sink you.

God's favor is upon you, and no viper can poison the source of your power.

Shake free, my friend, from all that holds you back.

You made it to Rome!

Your time is now!

SHAKE FREE . . . FROM ANYTHING HOLDING YOU BACK

You have come so far and have seen God do many miraculous things in your life. As we conclude our time together, I leave you with a few final questions to help you reflect on where you've been, where you are, and where God is leading you next. Godspeed on your journey!

1. Do you believe you've arrived in your Rome, or are you still on your way? What may be holding you back and preventing you from reaching the destination where you know God wants you to be?

2. Are you waiting on God to move a mountain that he wants you to climb? What challenge have you been avoiding that now must be conquered in order for you to continue your journey of faith toward Rome?

3. What else is slowing you down or holding you back from being all God made you to be? In the space that follows, list each barrier that comes to mind and ask God's Spirit to give you wisdom and guidance about your next steps of faith. Trust that the Lord will give you the strength and stamina you need to face anything before you. Thank you, Jesus. Hallelujah!

Dear God, thank you for bringing me to where I am right now! I praise you for all the ways you have miraculously intervened— what I've seen and what has gone unseen—to help me arrive at this place. As Paul did on his journey to Rome, allow me to shake free of every obstacle and overcome every barrier that would prevent me from fulfilling the destiny you have for me, Lord. I can't wait to see where you will lead me next. Bind the Enemy from hindering my efforts as I boldly step out to be the person you want me to be. I'm so grateful for the life you've given me and the special purpose placed in my heart. Onward and upward! Amen.

Acknowledgments

I want to thank Dudley Delffs for partnering with me in framing and contextualizing this powerful story. You are amazing!

Bruce Nygren of WaterBrook, you are a rock star. Thank you for your friendship, for believing in me, and for taking this vision and sharing it with the world.

I also want to thank my agent, Shannon Marven of Dupree Miller and Associates. Your insights and instincts have been a fountain of wisdom at every step of the journey, and I am forever grateful.

About the Author

Rev. Dr. Samuel Rodriguez is the president of the National Hispanic Christian Leadership Conference, identified by *Time, The New York Times, The Wall Street Journal, Christianity Today,* CNN, and other media organizations as America's largest and most influential Hispanic/Latino Christian organization. Rodriguez has been named on multiple lists of influencers in America.

An award-winning and best-selling author, Rodriguez contributes to many prominent publications. He is the author of *Be Light* and *The Lamb's Agenda* and coauthor of *When Faith Catches Fire,* with Dr. Robert Crosby.

In January 2013 Rodriguez was the first Latino to deliver the keynote address at the Martin Luther King Jr. Annual Commemorative Service at Ebenezer Baptist Church in Atlanta. In 2017 he became the first Hispanic evangelical leader to deliver an invocation at a presidential inauguration.

Rodriguez has worked with and advised President George W. Bush, President Barack Obama, and President Donald Trump. He served on President Obama's White House Task Force on Fatherhood and Healthy Families, and he frequently meets and consults with members of both parties in Congress on agenda items including immigration reform, racial reconciliation, and criminal justice reform.

Rodriguez earned his master's degree in educational leadership from Lehigh University and has received honorary doctorates from Baptist University of the Américas and Northwest University. He has been an Assemblies of God ordained minister since the age of twenty-three.